Revolutionary States, Leaders, and Foreign Relations

Revolutionary States, Leaders, and Foreign Relations

A Comparative Study of China, Cuba, and Iran

Houman A. Sadri

Foreword by R. K. Ramazani

Westport, Connecticut
London

Library of Congress Cataloging-in-Publication Data

Sadri, Houman A.
    Revolutionary states, leaders, and foreign relations : a
comparative study of China, Cuba, and Iran / Houman A. Sadri ;
foreword by R. K. Ramazani.
        p.   cm.
    Includes bibliographical references and index.
    ISBN 0-275-95321-1 (alk. paper)
    1. International relations. 2. Revolutionaries. 3. Comparative
government. 4. Iran—Foreign relations—1979– 5. China—Foreign
relations—1949– 6. Cuba—Foreign relations—1959– I. Title.
JX1395.S18   1997
327.1′01—dc20   96–32468

British Library Cataloguing in Publication Data is available.

Library of Congress Catalog Card Number: 96–32468
ISBN: 0-275-95321-1

First published in 1997

Praeger Publishers, 88 Post Road West, Westport, CT 06881
An imprint of Greenwood Publishing Group, Inc.

Printed in the United States of America

The paper used in this book complies with the
Permanent Paper Standard issued by the National
Information Standards Organization (Z39.48–1984).

10 9 8 7 6 5 4 3 2 1

This book is dedicated to my
parents, Khosrow and Zoheida,
who sowed the seeds of
knowledge in their
four children and
taught us that the best
investment in life is
one in education.
Neda, Negar, Sam, and I
are indebted to you forever.

CONTENTS

FOREWORD

The contribution of Professor Sadri's study may be assessed from three perspectives. First, his plea for a better understanding of the behavior of revolutionary states, especially those of the Third World, is fully compatible with the age-old awareness in the political science community of the general need to bridge the persistent gap between the study of comparative politics and international relations. More than three decades ago, I reiterated this need in suggesting the "dynamic triangular interaction" approach to the study of foreign policy and applied it to the foreign policy of Iran. Quincy Wright, who was then the preeminent American specialist on international relations and law, considered my study to be a "a basis for a theory of international politics and particularly of the foreign policy of small states." I consider Sadri's study helpful in narrowing the divide between the literature on revolution and on international relations.

Second, Sadri strikes a healthy balance in comparing the foreign policy behavior of China, Cuba and Iran in the first decade after revolution in terms of differences and similarities. He points out the differences in size and resources, military capability, character of non-alignment strategies, institutions, and leadership, although the greatest emphasis is placed on the phenomenon of leadership. He also outlines similarities such as radical departure of revolutionary regimes from the foreign policy orientation of the old regimes, particularly in relations with the United States, the common element of "nationalism" as a major influence in foreign policy making in spite of Communist and Islamist ideologies at work, and the rise of moderating influences in the shaping of foreign policy.

Regarding this latter observation, Sadri seems to be closer to the position of Kenneth N. Waltz who, like other neorealists, claims that revolutionary states will be "socialized" to the international system rather than to Henry Kissinger, who like other classical realists, generally views revolutionary regimes as a threat to the system. In his new landmark study, Revolution and War, Stephen M. Walt contends that the Waltzian view is only "partly correct," particularly as judged by the persistence of Soviet, Chinese and Iranian Revolutionary objectives far longer than was necessary.

Finally, although Sadri does not specifically deal with the implications of his study for future American policy toward revolutionary regimes, his plea for a better understanding of their foreign policy behavior may be interpreted as implying that there is a need for a more sophisticated and nuanced U.S. policy. Our friends and allies everywhere, especially in Europe, strongly disagree with hostile U.S. policies toward these states. They advocate a policy of "critical engagement," not appeasement, as a constructive way of moderating these regimes' foreign policy positions because their greater involvement in the international system rather than isolation, would constrain their behavior. It would also strengthen the hands of moderate elements within revolutionary societies. On the contrary, a belligerent policy will play into the hands of the more radical factions and will eventually hurt the United States' national interest.

R. K. Ramazani
University of Virginia

PREFACE

The original idea behind this work dates to my days as a young foreign student in the United States in the late 1970s. In fact, this book can be viewed as a product of that naive student's endeavors to satisfy his curiosity. This curiosity stemmed from puzzlement over the dynamic nature and process of the 1979 Iranian Revolution with its global impacts. As an individual whose life was touched deeply by this revolution, I was astonished by how rapidly a revolution can change the nature of relations among states, especially between small and great powers. Interested in international relations, I wondered why a revolution would make a foe out of a friendly state and vice versa. It was interesting for me to observe how the positive image of my native land altered almost overnight in America. This change in attitude toward Iran was clear not only in statements made by American government officials, but also in pictures portrayed by the media and by general public sentiment. In short, one day Tehran and Washington were allies and the next they were mortal enemies in search of an opportunity to destroy one another. Was such a conclusion accurate? Even if it were, why? Another question ringing in my mind was: who was at fault?

This personal fascination with the impact of revolutions eventually led to an academic interest in revolutionary states, especially their foreign relations. At the university level, I had a variety of choices among courses about revolutions offered by professors in various disciplines. I took history, political science, and sociology classes, but they all shared a focus on mainly domestic rather than foreign dimensions of revolutions. These courses were excellent in providing theoretical and historical knowledge about how major revolutions come about, the main characteristics of each, and how they institutionalize over time, yet neglected the foreign relations of revolutionary states. This made me even more eager to learn about the subject in any way that I could. I must admit that the more I searched and read, the more I realized that the literature on this topic is relatively weak, in comparison to the vast and comprehensive body of works that concentrates on the internal aspects of revolutions, especially "great" revolutions.

In any case, although the literature of revolutions is rich in theories and concepts coined by a variety of scholars, it has not offered reliable guidelines for predicting the next revolution. Nor has it been instrumental in estimating the behavior of most revolutionary states. In fact, one may argue that experts of revolutions and ordinary citizen alike are often caught by surprise when revolutions occur in the wake of most revolutionary political developments.

In addition to my inquisitiveness about the topic, an observation that I had soon after arriving to this country has been related to this endeavor. I learned that an average American is apolitical and innocent about world affairs in many respects. The latter characteristic, I found to be related to a lack of knowledge about the global environment as well as a lack of genuine interest in other countries. This was fascinating for me because many people give lip service to the phrase "We are now living in a global village." Well, how could we live in a global village and not know much about other cultures and countries in this shrinking world? This ignorance is especially significant now that the United States is the only superpower, and it is expected to act in a variety of capacities throughout the world.

Generally speaking, I have noticed that many non-Americans, even Europeans, know more about America than Americans know about other countries and cultures. In fact, I found most Americans to have an introverted view of the sociopolitical issues at hand. The majority prefer to talk about sports, movies, ways to make money, or anything other than politics. They usually talk about politics when presidential races dominate the media or during an economic or political crisis. Even when they do talk politics, the issues are mainly domestic, not foreign in nature.

There are most likely several reasons for Americans' general lack of political knowledge about other countries. As the nationals of the most powerful, wealthiest, and most technologically advanced society, many may feel unaffected by other states. Consequently, they have little need to concern themselves with the politics of the developing world or to become acquainted with customs of other cultures. Especially in the age of political correctness, many Americans may also shy away from political topics because they aim to avoid controversy. The fear of how to deal with certain countries might be particularly significant within certain circles where there are either foreign policy hawkish or dovish activists. The outcome could be simple avoidance of certain explosive topics on politics and foreign relations inside and outside the classroom structure.

Conversely, I have found that citizens of other countries resemble "political animals." In Europe, for instance, there is no way to avoid talking about politics, especially foreign relations. The same is true in developing countries, even though the citizens are protective of their privacy and avoid conversing about issues that could result in washing someone else's dirty laundry in public. In any case, with family one talks politics. With friends one talks politics. In lines to buy groceries one talks politics. In a taxi, the driver talks about politics and how other countries relate to domestic matters. I believe it would benefit the United States for its citizens to be similarly interested in and knowledgeable about events outside their own backyard.

Thus, the task of this book is twofold: to satisfy my own academic curiosity and to inform others that we live in a transitional period, when naivety and isolationist tendencies could be dangerous and counterproductive to world order and peace. There is a danger that internal conflicts (like coups and revolutions) can lead to external ones, like wars.

In the aftermath of World War II, revolutions upset a surprisingly large number of developing counties, among them Afghanistan, Algeria, Cambodia, China, Cuba, Ethiopia, Iran, Iraq, Mozambique, and Nicaragua, to name a few. Revolutionary regimes in these culturally and geographically diverse states came to power through different routes. Once in power, however, they had remarkably similar ideas about how to conduct their foreign relations with other states, particularly the great powers. This work illustrates common patterns in their behavior and how such behavior relates to the types of leadership.

This book fits into a "comparative international relations" category, to borrow one of James Rosenau's phrases. It is a study of three prominent revolutionary states from the developing world during a relatively compressed period of time, 1945 to 1990. During this crucial period that coincided with the Cold War, revolutionary leaders in countries as disparate as giant China, tiny Cuba, and ancient Iran attempted to radically remake their societies and the way in which they associate with other states. What can be concluded about the foreign policy goals and records of these regimes during the first formidable decade of their existence? In formulating a reply, my aim here is to illuminate and give meaning to the drama of these revolutionary states and to solicit appreciation for the many hopes and tragedies they spawned.

In the post-Watergate era, we live in a society that is increasingly concerned about the abuse of power by government officials. Today there is more scrutiny of public officials and government conduct than during any other period in the history of this country. In such an environment, an absence of public knowledge concerning the political histories of other societies and how the United States has been associated with them traditionally can permit an administration to exercise excessive influence over the citizenry's perception of its actions in foreign lands. This ability could lead to an abuse of power by the government. For instance, it is conceivable that ordinary Americans would have reacted differently to events in China, Cuba, and Iran, if they had clear and comprehensive knowledge of the U.S. role in the affairs of these countries prior to their revolutions and of American foreign policy toward them in the post-revolutionary periods.

Like many educational institutions, the media, for the most part, fell short of providing adequate information to the public about other societies and how the United States has traditionally related to them. Most people obtain news from television stations that in the process of competing for advertising dollars aim to maximize viewer ratings. This is often done by major networks giving lower priority to programs dealing with political topics about world affairs in favor of sitcoms, sports events, and game shows during prime time hours. The exception to this rule is programming during wartime or global crises. The lighter side of television programming and media focus is appealing to most American viewers.

There are, however, individuals who display a strong interest in learning about political events, issues, and conflicts around the world. They are not limited to members of academia, think tanks, and governmental agencies. An increasing number of mostly younger individuals are concerned with issues beyond the borders of this country. They recognize that it is becoming more difficult to draw a line between national and international issues. The growth of international non-governmental organizations (NGOs) is an indicator of the growth of this group. These interested people are particularly growing in numbers within colleges and universities, where I have been fortunate to observe them and their activities. Especially since the end of the Cold War, some of these individuals have begun to question traditional assumptions about lands beyond our borders and about the ends and means of U.S. foreign policy. It is mainly for this group of future leaders that this work exists. In addition to my attempt to reach out to such individuals, I sincerely hope that others, experts and non-experts alike, who chance upon this book will also benefit from the discussion and findings about the foreign relations of revolutionary states.

The list of those who played a significant role in the completion of this book is long and includes my instructors, graduate student peers, fellow faculty members in Florida, and students in Virginia and Florida. First of all, I would like to thank professors R. K. Ramazani and Inis L. Claude, Jr., who tirelessly mentored me during my graduate program at the University of Virginia. Their scholarly accomplishments and mentorship were the major factors in my deciding to pursue a doctorate in international relations at the Woodrow Wilson Department of Government and Foreign Affairs at UVA. Even after my graduation, they continued to be supportive and generous with their time and energy in assisting me to be a more objective, careful, and thorough student of foreign relations. I am grateful to the Thomas Jefferson Foundation in Charlottesville, Virginia for awarding me a generous research fellowship, without which the primary research for this work would not have been financially possible.

I would also like to thank all of my colleagues from Arizona, Virginia, and Florida for taking time to discuss with me different aspects and sections of this project in person and over wires. I am especially indebted to my colleagues at the University of Central Florida for their support, without which I could not have completed the job. My chairman, Robert Bledsoe, provided me with flexible schedules and the necessary equipment. I benefitted from the comments of Roger Handberg, who has served as my departmental mentor. Trudi Morales, who teaches the revolution course in our department, shared with me her insights and advised me accordingly. I also appreciate the efforts of Roger Simmons and Nick Buzmore from the UCF library for granting me respectively the necessary facility and the required resources to actually complete the manuscript.

I wish to thank all those students, both undergraduate and graduate, who have taken my international relations courses or worked with me on individual projects over the last few years. Little did they know that they were being presented with a work in progress, but their demands for clarity and detail certainly challenged me to become a better communicator and a more thorough student of foreign relations. In particular, my graduate student assistant, Brad Paul, helped a great deal to locate missing information in the endnotes. I am thankful for his resourcefulness and assistance.

I owe a personal debt to my publisher, James Dunton, who helped me to develop this volume by accepting my proposal, encouraging my efforts, and providing sound advice at important points along the way. Also, I sincerely thank my production editor David Palmer, who played a key role in keeping this project on schedule.

Last but certainly not least, I am grateful for the assistance of my friend Pamela Harris in editing, organizing, and preparing this manuscript. Her cheerful disposition and careful attention to detail made the often laborious task of revision a pleasure.

Given all this assistance, advice, and encouragement, I wish I could assert that the book is now without flaws. I sometimes stubbornly followed my prior path, despite the suggestions of friends and colleagues. Consequently, I take full responsibility for any errors of analysis or fact.

Houman A. Sadri

Revolutionary States, Leaders, and Foreign Relations

INTRODUCTION

Revolutions, great or small, have always been a fascinating subject for policy makers, experts, and educators alike. This is due in part to their sense of novelty and in part to their chaotic characteristics. The literature of revolutions is not only multidisciplinary in context, but also rich in concepts, theories, and models proposed by scholars who have employed diverse methods of analysis. Moreover, the literature is extensive for it covers a variety of issues, including the nature, causes, and impacts of revolutions, and accounts for numerous conditions and parameters.

Governments born from revolutions are often subject to scrutiny by foreign and domestic observers interested in the behavior of revolutionary regimes. Since the American Revolution, most outside observers of revolutions tend to be more cautious, critical, or pessimistic about the nature and behavior of revolutionary states, particularly in the infancy period of the regime. During the American Revolution, British writings on U.S. affairs included many examples of these types of observations. Conversely, most internal observers of revolutionary states tend to present a more bold, supportive, or optimistic view of their own revolutionary regime. Both positive and negative perspectives of revolutionary states are necessary for an international affairs student who aims to gain a more balanced and comprehensive understanding of the topic at hand.

Building on the rich literature of revolutions, *Revolutionary States, Leaders, and Foreign Relations* describes the nature and role of revolutionary leaders and explains their impact on the foreign relations of three prominent developing countries, China, Cuba, and Iran, during the first formidable decade following their revolutions. In so doing, this book addresses four fundamental questions about revolutionary leaders and the foreign policies they pursue. What are the types of revolutionary leaders, based upon their characteristics, styles, goals, and means? Which types of leaders lean toward which types of policies? How do these policies influence relations between revolutionary states and the Great Powers, especially the United States, in the New World Order? What do these case studies suggest about the behavior of other revolutionary states?

In an increasingly interdependent world, one cannot ignore the conflictual behavior of any state, since it adversely affects world order, peace, and security.[1] Most experts suggest that the great Revolutions create regimes that are often conflictual in conducting their foreign relations, particularly since they all attempt to export their revolutions in one way or another. In particular, the leaders of revolutionary Iran, Cuba, and China have defied the United States in many respects even in the absence of the Soviet Union, which has forced them to rethink their domestic and foreign policy priorities. In fact, most policy makers and scholars agree that the two common characteristics of revolutionary states are the conflictual and unpredictable nature of their foreign policy behavior.

Contrary to this stereotype, I intend to illustrate that the behavior of revolutionary states is not as irregular, irrational, or unpredictable as many assume and that there are identifiable patterns in the foreign relations of these so-called unpredictable regimes. The case studies covered here clearly show similarities in the formulation and implementation of foreign policy among a variety of revolutionary states despite significant differences in their cultural, historical, and geographical settings. The general trend indicates that the foreign relations of these states began with a two-track policy, which turned to a conflictual strategy and then led to a more conciliatory policy during the first decade of the new regime. This initial period is significant for the revolution is not yet institutionalized, and the leaders have a major impact on the policymaking process.

This work presents an unconventional view of the foreign relations patterns of revolutionary states, based upon a combination of new and old observations. Although this book relies on some recent sources, I have made a special effort to include earlier works and to emphasize relevant observations made in secondary sources published during the Cold War era. Many such observations, however, did not receive the attention they well deserved at the time of their publication. Thus, I have organized the ideas presented by a variety of experts in the field and made sure to give credit where it is due. In sum, what is new about this work is not necessarily the presentation of new data, but a fresh way of looking at existing information.

References to China's, Cuba's, and Iran's so-called unexpected or unpredictable policy, however, imply that our understanding of the behavior of these revolutionary states is far from complete. Since the Cold War is no longer tainting our policy analysis, we need to reassess our knowledge about the formulation and implementation of their foreign relations from a different policy perspective. Responding to this need, I explain the foreign relations of these revolutionary developing countries based upon their own interpretation of events for the most part, short of justifying or apologizing for their policy misconduct.

Students of revolutions can have a more comprehensive understanding of the behavior of revolutionary regimes if they do not analyze it solely from a Western perspective. This reassessment is especially possible now due to two factors. First, our analytical perception is no longer contaminated with a zero-sum Cold War thinking. The second factor is the availability of new primary and secondary sources. Some government records in Russia and America have been declassified. Also a few recent publications question some traditional assumptions about the foreign relations of China, Cuba, and Iran and the real intentions of their prominent leaders.

The scope of this book is limited to the first decade following each revolution because a comprehensive analysis of the foreign relations of all three revolutionary states would require much more extensive study from a historical perspective. My main purpose is to question the validity of certain assumptions about these revolutionary states and to reexamine our general knowledge of Chinese, Cuban, and Iranian foreign relations during the infancy period of their revolutions. By adding to the traditional Western-oriented analysis of this crucial period a non-Western perspective, whether "Chinacentric," Cubacentric," or "Irancentric" perspectives, we will gain a more comprehensive understanding of the intricacies of the present-day foreign policies of Beijing, Havana, and Tehran, despite some changes in both their domestic and international conditions.

This book is suitable for a variety of readers. For policymakers the outlined foreign relations patterns ease the process of anticipating the behavior of contemporary and perhaps future revolutionary regimes. This is important as it contributes to improved communication with different types of revolutionary leaders and could lead to minimizing unwanted conflict in either a bilateral or multilateral context.

For scholars the book narrows the gap in the literature of leadership and policy studies. First, although there are a few fine biographical studies of Fidel Castro, Ayatollah Khomeini, and Mao Zedong,[2] experts have focused little attention on comparing the character, role, and style of such leaders in order to suggest a conceptual framework for analyzing their behavior. There exist two major studies of leadership that are useful from a comparative perspective: one by James MacGregor Burns and the other by Marvin Folkertsma. These studies, however, do not address the objectives of my book for Burns's work is mainly concerned with the relationship between the leaders and their followers in a Western context and the latter study suggests four types of leaders according to their world view and provides American and European examples.[3] Moreover, there are no works similar to James Barber's *The Presidential Character* which focuses on the influence of the personality and style of leaders of the developing world on policymaking.[4] In this respect, this study is the first attempt to present a comparative leadership perspective concentrating only on the developing world.

A second unique feature of this book is its contribution to the field of policy studies. Although there is considerable literature on the Chinese, Cuban, and Iranian revolutions individually, there are few studies that carefully and exclusively analyze the impact of leadership on postrevolutionary foreign policy, and even fewer that approach the subject from a crosscultural perspective. In fact, there are no studies comparing the influence of leadership on the foreign policy of revolutionary states from East Asia, Latin America, and the Middle East combined.

These two distinguishing attributes of the study are valuable not only to policymakers and students of foreign policy and leadership studies, but also to area journalists who often want to know about general trends in politics. Moreover, this topic is salient as any major challenge to global peace in an increasingly interdependent world would most likely come from a revolutionary state, such as Cuba, Iran, Iraq, or North Korea, also referred to as rogue states by the Clinton Administration. Some current examples of such behaviors are North Korea's aim to develop nuclear weapons, Iran's intention to promote Islamic revolutions, Cuba's attempt to advance a socialist regime, and even China's policy to deter the pro-democracy movement in its sphere of influence, despite its leaning toward a market-oriented model of economic development. In fact, the very first major challenge to the New World Order came from a revolutionary state when Iraq invaded Kuwait and outraged members of the international community, particularly the Great Powers.

In this book, the involvement of revolutionary leaders in the policymaking process is studied from a combination of two perspectives: contextual and personal. The first emphasizes the domestic and international conditions under which leaders act.[5] The role of a revolutionary leader is determined according to the expectations of the Great Powers, the historical context of the state, the domestic political demands, and the socioeconomic conditions of the country at the time. Second, a personal perspective emphasizes the leader's character, world view, style, and the way in which his performance in a variety of settings is influenced by them.[6] I assess the attitudes, styles, and world views of prominent Chinese, Cuban, and Iranian leaders, particularly Fidel Castro, Carlos Rafael Rodriguez, Zhou Enlai, Mao Zedong, Ali Akbar Hashemi-Rafsanjani, and Ayatollah Khomeini. Each leader brought his own personal skills and political experience to the job and in doing so contributed to the manner in which his state performed under varied conditions. Hence, the study finds leadership to be a function of the interactive influences of environmental conditions and personal attributes.

The book shows that there are two general categories of revolutionary leaders, idealists and realists. The revolutionary idealists see the success of the revolution as a stepping stone in a series of upheavals against enemies, both inside and outside of the country. The anti-status quo rhetoric of the idealists often poses a threat to the national security of other states, especially in the first few years after the revolution. Generally, revolutionary idealists, like Mao and Khomeini, tend to romanticize the nature and effects of their revolution. They are also optimistic about their regime's ability to orchestrate similar revolutions in other countries.

This romanticism and optimism can, however, blind the idealist to essential facts. One example is whether or not the time and conditions for a similar revolution in other states are optimum. The most well known example of such a miscalculation was Ernesto Che Guevara's decision to leave Cuba for Bolivia to organize a revolution similar to that of Havana. He failed and was killed in the process by native Bolivians.[7]

Revolutionary realists are those leaders who understand realpolitik and the limits to the powers of their states. This group is often more familiar and concerned with the reaction of the international environment to their revolution and its consequences. Like the idealists, the realists also aim at exporting their revolution, albeit with different strategies. Instead of channeling resources to support terrorist and/or national liberation movements in other countries, their priority is building a model revolutionary state. They also realize that their country needs outside assistance for modernization and security. Consequently, they understand the importance of maintaining at least some diplomatic and economic relations with other countries, particularly with the Great Powers. Realists are also pragmatic enough to recognize that internationally isolating the country (like China in the early 1950s) does not pay off. Zhou Enlai and Deng Xiaoping are examples of revolutionary realists who worked against the isolationist tendencies in China. President Rafsanjani of Iran is another.

This work also demonstrates power politics at two different, but overlapping, dimensions: domestic and international. On the international level, it illustrates the interaction between the leaders of each revolutionary state and those of the Great Powers. At the domestic level, it reveals the power play between revolutionary realists and idealists in China, Cuba, and Iran. Finally, this book illustrates the interactions between domestic and international affairs. This task is important, for international and domestic concerns are merging in today's world in such a way that one observer has coined a new word, *intermestic*.[8]

Revolutionary States is made up of six chapters, beginning with a brief introductory chapter that presents the main concepts and perspectives of revolutionary leadership. It poses a series of analytical questions about the Chinese, Cuban, and Iranian revolutionary leaders and their foreign policy strategies and defines the major concepts used in this study. Chapter 2 describes the international environment in which the three revolutions occurred and their foreign relations developed. Focusing on the bipolar international structure, this section explains the reasons for the growth of an international political movement in the developing world, the Non-Alignment Movement (NAM). It also describes the elements and criteria of non-alignment, which served as a policy option for many developing countries, particularly revolutionary ones, during the Cold War era.

The next three chapters examine the impact of leadership on the foreign relations of each country in a case study format. Chapter 3 illustrates the role and impact of Chinese revolutionary leaders from the 1949 Revolution to 1959 (after the offshore islands crisis) on Chinese foreign affairs. Chapter 4 concentrates on the critical first decade of the Cuban Revolution, during which Castro survived the

Bay of Pigs and the 1962 missile crisis, until his foreign policy began to show signs of moderation in the late 1960s. The next chapter addresses the challenges that the leadership of Ayatollah Khomeini created for the Great Powers following the 1979 Revolution. This period is especially significant because it covers the triangular interactions among Moscow, Tehran, and Washington during the last decade of the Cold War.

The final chapter compares and contrasts predominant factors that explain the nature, scope, and trends of foreign relations of the three states. In this regard, I first focus on the differences among the experiences of the three revolutionary states. Then I concentrate on the similarities that these diverse groups of developing countries have shown in the conduct of their foreign policies. My discussion indicates that there are a number of factors that are worth emphasizing in the analysis. These factors can be used to understand and estimate the foreign policy behavior of these revolutionary states, in particular, and other revolutionary states in general. The chapter concludes by presenting how findings about the role, nature, and impact of revolutionary leaders on foreign policy trends during the Cold War apply to current conditions in the international community. Obviously, the shift in the structure of the international system from Cold War to post-Cold War has radically altered the international context of the policymaking process, especially among weak or developing states. Since the end of the Cold War, what some call the "political space" of most developing countries has significantly shifted. One should note that in the Cold War era, as a result of a world divided into two ideological camps, developing countries faced limited policy options, or "political space."[9]

Information to support the findings of this study was collected from a wide range of sources, predominantly secondary ones. I have utilized numerous articles and books from diverse perspectives, especially those representing the views of leaders of these revolutionary states. In addition, I have relied on some primary sources, such as government documents and data from international organizations.

NOTES

1. For an excellent analysis of the current changes in international relations and the role of the United States, see Inis L. Claude, Jr., *The United States in a Changing World*, The Annual Paley Lectures in American Culture and Civilization, The Hebrew University of Jerusalem, (Jerusalem: The Academon Press, 1993).

2. For classical studies about the personality of Castro, Khomeini, and Mao, see Jules Dubois, *Fidel Castro, Rebel, Liberator, or Dictator?* (Indianapolis: Bobbs-Merrill, 1959); Lucian W. Pye, *Mao Tse-tung: The Man in the Leader*, (New York: Basic Books, 1976); Farhang Rajaee, *Islamic Values and World View: Khomeyni on Man, the State, and International Politics*, (New York: University Press of America, 1983).

3. James MacGregor Burns, *Leadership* (New York: Harper and Row, 1978); and Marvin J. Folkertsma, Jr., *Ideology and Leadership* (Englewood Cliffs, N.J.: Prentice-Hall, 1988).

4. James David Barber, *Presidential Character*, 4th ed. (Englewood Cliffs, N.J.: Prentice-Hall, 1992).

5. Some notable examples include R. K. Ramazani, *Revolutionary Iran* (Baltimore, Md.: Johns Hopkins University Press, 1986); Edgar Snow, *Red Star Over China* (New York: Groves Press, 1968); and William Appleman Williams, *The U.S., Cuba, and Castro* (New York: Monthly Review Press, 1962).

6. Among well-known general studies are Harold D. Lasswell, *Psychopathology and Politics* (New York.: Viking Press, 1960); and James David Barber, *The Presidential Character*, 4th ed. (Englewood Cliffs, N.J.: Prentice-Hall, 1992).

7. John Dunn, *Modern Revolutions*, 2d. ed. (Cambridge: Cambridge University Press, 1989), 199-225, especially 207.

8. Bayless Manning, "The Congress, The Executive, and Intermestic Affairs," *Foreign Affairs* 57 (1979): 308-24.

9. For further discussion, see H. Michael Erismand and John M. Kirk, *Cuban Foreign Policy Confronts a New International Order*, (Boulder, Colo.: Lynne Rienner, 1991), 1-5.

1

TYPOLOGY AND TERMINOLOGY OF REVOLUTIONS

Much has been and continues to be written about revolutions, but there is no consensus among experts about definitions of concepts or about the process of revolution itself. In order to clarify the major assumption of this book, it is necessary to briefly define the terms that I use.

REVOLUTIONS AND THE REVOLUTIONARY STATE

All developing countries are not revolutionary in nature, and all revolutionary states are not part of the developing world. This statement is theoretically sound and has been practically accurate up to the demise of the Soviet Union. The former Soviet Union and its Eastern European allies were revolutionary in nature, but they were considered to be developed countries. Thus, the scope of this study is limited to those states that are both developing countries and members of an exclusive club —revolutionaries. Interestingly enough, all revolutionary developing countries have asserted that they pursue a foreign policy independently of the great powers. In many corners, this foreign relations strategy is known as non-alignment. The three states in this study—China, Cuba, and Iran—are all considered to be revolutionary states, although each is currently at a different stage in its economic and political development. These three developing countries have all, at one time or another, explicitly or implicitly accepted the principle of non-alignment. Thus, there is a philosophical connection between the concepts of revolution and non-alignment. Before analyzing this connection, however, I must examine the notions of revolution and revolutionary state.

Revolution is a nebulous term, one that is interpreted differently by different scholars. Crane Brinton, a well-known student of revolutions, stated that revolution is one of the "looser words" used by experts and non-experts alike.[1]

This book focuses on what many social scientists call the "Great Revolutions," which bring major changes to sociopolitical values, legal and political institutions, and leadership. This group of revolutions includes the 1949 Chinese, 1959 Cuban, 1789 French, 1979 Iranian, 1979 Nicaraguan, and 1917 Russian Revolutions. I have narrowed the scope of this study by concentrating on only three cases from prominent developing countries.

Let's begin our analysis of the concept of revolution by observing how dictionaries define the term. Webster defines revolution as "a sudden, radical, or complete change ... [or] ... a fundamental change in political organization ... [especially] the overthrow or renunciation of one government or ruler and the substitution of another by the governed."[2] The same source defines the term *revolutionary* as "constituting a revolution" or "tending to or promoting revolution."[3] From a political science perspective, the above definition is too general and rather vague. For example, it does not indicate who is the force behind a revolution—the elite or the masses. Nor does it mention anything about the political values involved in the revolutionary process.

I define revolutions as forceful attempts by the masses to bring about radical changes to the sociopolitical values, institutional system, and leadership in a short period of time. This type of change is always formalized by a new constitutional arrangement.[4] With this definition, I separate revolutions from such similar concepts as coups, civil wars, or wars of independence, which can also lead to a sudden change of government, but do not often have the same effects on the society as revolutions and revolutionaries.

In practice, revolutions require the use of force for they involve radical change. Some argue, however, that monumental change in a society can also occur peacefully. This view represents a minority position among most scholars of revolution, and it is well described by Lyford Edwards, who advocates that revolutionary change is "brought about not necessarily by force and violence."[5] Nevertheless, the majority of students of revolution admit that violence is an integral part of a revolution. One theorist summarizes the three major characteristics of any revolution: "revolutions are a form of massive, violent and rapid social change."[6] Not all violence produced by a revolution is revolutionary in nature, however, as Robert Dahl clearly explained: "When I read that looting T.V. sets from neighborhood stores is an act of revolutionary violence, I wonder whether politics and the theater are not converging—to the detriment of both."[7]

Some experts take an extreme position by arguing that it is not possible to separate the revolution from the violence. For instance, Chalmors Johnson stated that one method of analyzing "the concept of revolution is to examine it as a form of violence."[8] A revolutionary regime, therefore, is defined as a government that has gained political control through the use of naked force by the masses (not by the regular armed forces) and has succeeded in changing the sociopolitical values, legal and political institutions, and the leadership in a relatively short period of time. In fact, time is a vital variable in identifying a revolutionary regime. Because all political entities eventually, albeit gradually, change, one major element that separates a revolutionary regime from an evolutionary one is the difference in the amount of time it takes for the changes to occur. In addition to considering time, most students of revolutions agree that it is also important to examine the role of both internal and external violence in the behavior of revolutionary regimes. For example, many observers of Revolutionary China have suggested that China's belligerent foreign policy is a result of its internal problems. Andres Onate's empirical study illustrated that there was a moderate statistical relationship between total amount of internal conflict and the total amount of external conflict expressed by revolutionary China.[9]

THE ROLE OF REVOLUTIONARY LEADERS IN FOREIGN POLICY

Foreign policymaking is often done by institutions in developed countries but mostly by the leaders in developing countries, particularly revolutionary states.[10] Thus, the analysis of foreign relations of developing countries usually involves a closer examination of the leadership variable than does analysis of developed countries.[11] While not all revolutionary leaders participate in the decision-making process to the same degree, they agree that there is a need for change in their foreign policies to signify a break from previous foreign policy.

The issue of change in political, and, consequently, human behavior raises questions and academic debate about human nature. The roots of contending ideas about change and human nature can be traced to the seventeenth-century debate between the followers of Thomas Hobbes and the followers of John Locke. While Hobbes described human nature as fixed, universal, and evil, Locke portrayed it as flexible and capable of good. Like Locke, Jean Jacques Rousseau (1712 – 1778) also described human nature as flexible and capable of good. Rousseau argued that people gather in civil societies because they reach a point at which the difficulties of improving the quality of life surpass the resources available to each individual. Moreover, humans have come to understand that the primitive conditions of their existence are no longer tolerable, and they could perish if they do not change the manner of their existence. The contending views of Hobbes, along with those of Locke and Rousseau, formed the root of the realist-idealist debate.[12]

These two opposing characteristics of human nature necessarily result in two different types of states and two different types of leaders with very different missions.[13] The aggressive nature of the Hobbesian man requires a Leviathan state and strong leadership if man is to survive. Only a leader with absolute political power can control the evil nature of man and his behavior.[14] Locke assumed, on the other hand, that mankind is changeable by reason and experience and that he can control his own behavior. Consequently, the state should play a relatively benign role, and leaders should remain passive. The ideas of John Locke had the most significant influence on revolutionary Americans, among all revolutionaries in the world.[15]

It is not clear what makes an individual become revolutionary.[16] We are not sure why such individuals prefer to overthrow the government rather than reform it from within the system.[17] On the basis of their approaches toward foreign policy, however, we can divide revolutionary leaders into two general categories: idealists and realists. In time, many policy experts have used these categories in their analyses, although they have defined these terms in their own ways. This might raise a question for the reader about how the author defines each category.

IDEALISTS

Revolutionary Idealists

Revolutionary idealists are those who see the success of the revolution as a stepping-stone in a series of upheavals against enemies, both inside and outside the country. A large number of this group can be called internationalists in the sense that they particularly focus on the external setting. In contrast, a revolutionary nationalist has an inward-looking perspective. Revolutionary idealists are similar to internationalists in that they have an outward-looking perspective. Many challenge their international environments. Their anti-status quo rhetoric often poses a threat to the national security of other states, especially in the first few years after the revolution. Such internationalists include revolutionary leaders like Ernesto Che Guevara and Ali Akbar Mohtashami. The latter, I must add, is not as internationally well known as Che Guevara or Leon Trotsky. In Iran, however, he is one of the best-known revolutionary idealists and is often portrayed as anti-American by the Western media. In fact, he is not just anti-American, but anti-Western and was anti-Eastern (when there was an Eastern camp). A decade after the revolution, he was no longer an interior minister and had lost much of his political clout. In the 1990s he still questions the resumption of ties with the Western states, not just the United States.[18] On the tenth anniversary of the storming of the U.S. Embassy, Mohtashemi was the main speaker at the ceremony in the compound of the American Embassy. Revolutionary idealists, however, do not believe in an interdependent world. Along these lines, R. K. Ramazani stated: "Both revolutionary Russia and China tried to reject the concept of an interdependent world culture and both have ended up accepting it. They had no other choice; nor does revolutionary Iran."[19] For idealists, the revolutionary state must persist in using its revolutionary values in its foreign relations. They believe that time is working to their advantage and that sooner or later their revolution will spread elsewhere.

Generally, revolutionary idealists tend to romanticize the nature and effects of their revolution. The tendency toward romanticism is rooted in some of the intellectual sources of idealists, including Rousseau.[20] They are also optimistic about their ability to orchestrate similar revolutions in other countries, especially after they gain experience in executing a successful revolution. Idealists tend to be impatient when their ideas take longer to implement than anticipated or when the ideas in practice stray from their original goals.

This romanticism and optimism can, however, blind the idealist to essential facts. For example, when Che Guevara left Cuba for Bolivia to organize a revolution, he failed to consider a major difference in the makeup of the two countries: the large indigenous Indian population of Bolivia.[21] One can also argue that revolutionary idealists, an ingredient of any revolutionary leadership group, are simplistic and gullible in assuming that their revolution is exportable. They consider the exporting of the revolution the goal of any true revolutionary. They forget that a revolution that is to be legitimate, decisive, and successful must also be deeply rooted in the society, that will take up the revolt against the status quo.

Radical Revolutionary Idealists

Some revolutionary idealists have an extreme sense of the mission to export their revolution by any means, even by such interventionist tactics as directly supporting with training and arms the opposition military in other states. In fact, one can argue that these individuals concern themselves not with other governments or states, but with their nations. Similarly, they do not think in terms of official channels of communication or the relations between governments or states, but in terms of relations between people or nations. They often operate via unofficial channels. From a theoretical perspective, it is essential to recognize whether interstate or international relations are emphasized because they represent different types of world order. According to Inis Claude, Jr., there is a technical difference between interstate relations and international relations. While interstate relations refers to the relations between the government officials representing different societies, international relations is the contact between different nations or people from different parts of the world. These differences are rooted in the dissimilarities between the terms *state* and *nation*, which are often and incorrectly used interchangeably.[22]

I refer to such individuals as radical revolutionary idealists because they often attempt to organize a network to export their revolution, when the domestic conditions of their own state allow. What separates this group from other idealists is the means by which they attempt to export their revolutions. Radical idealists do not confine themselves to employing rhetoric and spiritual support as do most idealists. Rather, their goal is to send material support to groups with similar ideologies in other states. Or we may say, in comparison to other idealists, the radical idealists cannot be accused of having a "bark bigger than their bite."

Radical revolutionary idealists, like Mehdi Hashemi,[23] are not usually concerned with the negative international response to their crusade. They idealize a David and Goliath scenario and are convinced that their revolution can take on the world. For such individuals, the isolation of the country by major powers is unavoidable. In fact, they consider the isolation a blessing.

In order to achieve their goals, radical idealists often bypass their own governmental agencies, which they see as standing in their way. There are three reasons for this action. First, as the revolutionary fervor of the people and the regime gradually declines, the government's commitment to support other revolutionary movements becomes more rhetorical than actual. Second, the revolutionary government becomes overwhelmed with the ordinary duties of a typical government, having less time and resources to contribute to secondary goals, like aiding revolutionary movements beyond their borders. Finally, radical idealists are perceived as too impatient to wait for the right conditions to arrive in other states for similar revolutions to occur on their own.

Radical revolutionary idealists, however, are eager to change the world and begin a political campaign to take on the world. Repeatedly, the message of such individuals is that they have the only country with true independence, freedom, policy, and government and that other countries should follow their example, even if motivated by force.

REVOLUTIONARY REALISTS

Revolutionary realists are those leaders who understand realpolitik and the limits to the power of their revolutionary states. This group is more familiar with and concerned about the reaction of the international environment to their revolution and its consequences. Like the idealists, the realists also aim to export their revolution. Their strategy, however, is different. Instead of channeling resources to support national liberation movements, their priority is to build their own country into a model revolutionary state. They also realize that their country needs outside assistance for modernization. Consequently, they understand the importance of maintaining healthy diplomatic and economic relations with other countries, particularly with those who have advanced technology. From this perspective, although the realists are also revolutionaries, they are more concerned with the "bread and butter" issues. They are also more inclined to deal with problems of national, rather than of international, concern. This may be so because they tend to be pessimistic about the ability of their state to change the world. Thus, one must consider them more nationalist than internationalist.

Realists are also pragmatic enough to realize that internationally isolating the country does not pay off, as China's experience in the early 1950s illustrated. Deng Xiaoping is an example of a revolutionary realist who worked against the isolationist tendencies in Chinese foreign policy. In the post–1977 period, his emerging realpolitik, in a new version of the "three world theory," contradicted the moralistic and radical policies followed by Mao during the first period of the revolutionary regime.[24]

One may hypothesize that the more inward the goals and perspectives of the leaders, the less likely a revolutionary country is to face international opposition to its foreign policy. Revolutionary realists—for example Hashemi-Rafsanjani—are more pragmatic leaders. Concerned with the mounting pressures of economic development and war reconstruction efforts, Rafsanjani even advocated using foreign experts and contractors when similar services are not available domestically.[25] Rafsanjani's view deviated from the norm, for the general public and most revolutionary leaders were suspicious of the role and impact of foreign advisers due to experiences prior to the revolution.

SUMMARY

The tone of the foreign policy of a new regime is directly affected by whomever sets the policy agenda. The idealists are related to a more confrontational foreign policy and the realists a less confrontational policy. Thus, if a state that needs to deal with a revolutionary country can determine from its foreign policy trends who is swaying the policymaking, the state will then be in a position to better determine its course of action or reaction to the signals of a revolutionary regime.

Regardless of their differences, both revolutionary realists and idealists agree on the need for a fresh approach to the foreign relations of the new regime. Considering the pervasive image of the old regime as weak, inadequate, and/or dependent on foreign powers, most revolutionary leaders find a non-alignment strategy to be a suitable alternative, not only for their domestic image but also for their international reputation. Thus, the concept of non-alignment serves both the national and international political necessities of a revolutionary regime.

It should not be surprising, therefore, that in developing countries most revolutionary regimes, soon after the success of their revolutions, have declared non-alignment as the major principle of their foreign relations.

NOTES

1. Crane Brinton, *The Anatomy of Revolution* (New York: Vintage Books, 1965; first published in 1938), 3.

2. *Webster's New Collegiate Dictionary* (Springfield, Mass.: G. and C. Merriam, 1973), 992.

3. Ibid.

4. David L. Sills, ed., *International Encyclopedia of the Social* Sciences, Vol. 13 (New York: Macmillan and the Free Press, 1968), 501.

5. Lyford P. Edwards, *The Natural History of Revolution* (Chicago: University of Chicago Press, 1970; first published in 1927), 2.

6. John Dunn, *Modern Revolutions* (Cambridge: University Press, 1972), 13.

7. Robert Dahl, *After the Revolution?: Authority in a Good Society* (New Haven, Conn.: Yale University Press, 1970), 4.

8. Chalmors Johnson, *Revolutionary Change* (Stanford, Calif.: Stanford University Press, 1966), 7.

9. Andres Onate, "The Conflict Interactions of the People's Republic of China, 1950-1970," *Journal of Conflict Resolution* 18 (December 1974): 578 - 94.

10. See Charles W. Kegley, Jr. and Eugene R. Wittkopf, eds., *The Domestic Sources of American Foreign Policy: Insights and Evidence* (New York: St. Martin's Press, 1988), especially chapters 9 and 12. Also see John T. Rourke, *Making Foreign Policy: United States, Soviet Union, and China* (Pacific Grove, Calif.: Brooks/Cole, 1990), especially chapters 6 to 9.

11. See Philip Wilson Bonsal, *Cuba, Castro, and the United States* (Pittsburgh: University of Pittsburgh Press, 1971). Also see Robert S. Elegant, *Mao's Great Revolution* (New York: World Publishing, 1971.)

12. For Rousseau's perspective on this, see Jean Jacques Rousseau, "The Social Contract", *Rousseau's Political Writings*, eds. Alan Ritter and Julia Conaway Bondanella (New York: W.W. Norton, 1988; first published in 1762).

13. For a detailed comparison between these contending ideas, see Michael Walzer, *The Revolution of the Saints* (Cambridge: Harvard University Press, 1965).

14. Thomas Hobbes, *Leviathan* (Indianapolis: Bobbs-Merrill Educational Publishing, 1958); *Leviathan* was originally published in 1651.

15. The ideas of John Locke had a significant influence on revolutionary Americans. For more information, see Bernard Bailyn, The Ideological Origins of the American Revolution (Cambridge: Harvard University Press, 1967).

16. Lawrence Stone, "Theories of Revolution," *World Politics* 17 (January 1966): 168.

17. James E. Dougherty and Robert L. Pfaltzgraff, Jr., *Contending Theories of International Relations*, 3d ed. (New York: Harper and Row, 1990), 330.

18. *FBIS*, (7 February 1989). *Washington Post*, (5 November 1989). *FBIS*, (6 November 1989).

19. R. K. Ramazani, "Iran's Foreign Policy: Contending Orientations," in *Iran's Revolution: The Search for Consensus,* ed. R. K. Ramazani   (Bloomington: Indiana University Press, 1990), 65.

20. See Irving Babbitt, *Rousseau and Romanticism* (Boston: Houghton Mifflin., 1947).

21. John Dunn, *Modern Revolutions* 2d ed (Cambridge: Cambridge University Press, 1989), 207.

22. Author's personal interview with Professor Inis Claude, Jr., University of Virginia, Charlottesville, VA (Fall 1986).

23. For information on the activities of Hashemi, see Eric Hooglund's section on "Concept of Export of Revolution" in *Iran: A Country Study*, ed. Helen Metz (Washington, D.C.: U.S. Government Printing Office), 222-24.

24. Carol Lee Hamrin, "Domestic Components and China's Evolving Three World Theory," in *China & the Third World*, eds. Lillian Craig Harris and Robert L. Worden (Dover, Mass.: Auburn House, 1986), 42.

25. Richard Cottam, "Inside Revolutionary Iran," in Ramazani, ed., *Iran's Revolution*, 21.

2

NON-ALIGNMENT AS A
FOREIGN POLICY STRATEGY

Revolutionary states always emphasize their autonomy in the policymaking process. Independent policymaking has been traditionally associated with the concept of non-alignment in developing countries, particularly revolutionary regimes. This concept is a contribution of the Non-Alignment Movement (NAM) to international politics. In its thirty-five year history, NAM has never clearly and comprehensively defined this concept.

Some officials of lesser developed countries and some well-respected experts, however, have discounted the need for an authoritative and precise definition of non-alignment. Leo Mates, for example, maintained that there is virtue in not insisting on a single definition of the term. He argued that the traditional method of a common stand based upon a clearly written platform of a political community does not apply to non-alignment. He added: "All this is understandable, since the movement of the non-aligned countries is something new in international relations, not only because of a common platform, but also because of the form of cooperation among a large number of generally dissimilar countries."[1]

The response of one critic, M. S. Rajan, to this argument was:

The membership of the United Nations is even more diverse than that of the non-aligned movement, and yet the Preamble and the Purposes and Principles were considered essential to be incorporated in the U.N. Charter. Secondly, precisely because non-alignment is a new foreign policy choice, there is, a fortiori, a need for a definition of the policy; without a definition the new policy is likely to be (and it has in fact been) misunderstood and misrepresented from time to time in terms of the traditional foreign policy choices.[2]

The lack of a clear definition for non-alignment by NAM is not due to a lack of interest but to unbridgeable differences among member states, especially revolutionary and moderate ones. In 1973, at the fourth Summit of the Heads of States of Non-Aligned Countries, the revolutionary Libyans asked for a "new definition or stricter interpretation" of the term *non-alignment*. The conference, however, put aside the issue of definition from its agenda because of a lack of consensus on its inclusion. In the 1979 summit conference, avoiding the same issue resulted in Burma's formal withdrawal from the movement.[3] Thus, NAM has resisted the calls for a single definition not because the concept of non-alignment is meaningless or cannot be defined, but because of the lack of agreement on a single definition by all NAM members. Leo Mates clearly illustrated this problem when he stated:

It is not unreasonable to say that there are as many definitions of non-alignment as there are non-aligned countries and possibly even more ... In a certain sense, it can be said that the policy of non-alignment has permanently been undergoing definition, re-examination, and criticism while resisting arbitrary assessment.[4]

We can gain a better idea of why there is no definition for non-alignment by looking at the formation of the movement.

THE ORIGIN OF NON-ALIGNMENT

The Second World War brought two major changes to international politics and consequently led to the emergence of non-alignment as both a movement and a foreign policy strategy. The first change was the appearance of Washington and Moscow as the two predominant, contending powerhouses. These two major powers represented diametrically opposed sociopolitical value systems, and each believed its own ideology to be superior. This international phenomenon, known as bipolarity, ruled the long Cold War years, during which the revolutions of the three case study countries took place.[5]

The other important change was the collapse of old colonial systems in Japan and Europe. This collapse facilitated the process of independence for colonial territories in Asia and Africa. These newly independent states were emerging in an international environment dominated by ideological rivalry of the Cold War, a direct result of the activities of the superpowers. Some blamed the start of the Cold War on the United States, while others maintained that the Soviet Union was responsible. For the purposes of this study, the origins of the Cold War are not significant—only the fact that it existed.[6]

The newly emergent states constituted the bulk of what became known as the Third World. The latter consists of a large number of small and medium sized states with diverse socioeconomic and political backgrounds. These states were called Third World because they were neither a member of the First World (led by America) nor the Second World (led by Russia). In their foreign policies, the majority of Third World countries shared the goal of avoiding the superpower rivalry. To achieve this goal, these states employed non-alignment as a strategy in conducting their foreign relations. This was particularly true for revolutionary states, at least in their rhetoric. In brief, this strategy meant avoiding a military alliance with either superpower against the other. From this beginning, some Third World states that pursued non-alignment in their foreign relations formed a loose international alliance that became known as the Non-Aligned Movement.[7]

Now that we know how non-alignment generally came about, one may ask what distinguishes non-alignment from the well-known concept of neutrality in international relations. Contrary to the general assumption, the concepts of non-alignment and neutrality are not interchangeable. Their differences hinge on the nature, scope, and function of each concept. Their main difference is that they are associated with two separate academic disciplines—law and politics. Neutrality is usually used in a legal context, while non-alignment is studied as a political position.

WHAT IS NEUTRALITY?

Neutrality is a noun from the adjective *neutral*, which means "not engaged on either side" or "neither one thing nor the other."[8] The concept of neutrality indicates a policy sought during a state of belligerence when a third party decides not to participate on the side of either belligerent in a conflict, especially a war.

It is important to mention that neutrality, as we know it, is a by-product of the modern state system. Neutrality has not always had a positive connotation. For instance, it was not welcomed in Europe during the Middle Ages because of the belief in universally valid laws and an absolute sense of justice.[9] Conflicts were assumed to be between right and wrong or good and evil. It was morally unacceptable to be indifferent about what was right or good.

Neutrality became acceptable only when the ideas of natural law, universally divine standards, and the just war began to be questioned. The practice of neutrality was fully established after the concept of state sovereignty became accepted in the international system. Thus, there is a relationship between the concepts of sovereignty and neutrality.[10] Whenever state sovereignty stands firm in the world community, there is also room for neutrality. On the contrary, whenever sovereignty does not stand on firm ground because of the claims of universal truths based on ideology or religion, then neutrality becomes either unacceptable, immoral, or impractical.[11]

Neutrality is a legal position, and the literature of international law is rich with customs, judicial rulings, treaties, and legal precedents concerning neutrality that date to the seventeenth century. Neutrality laws clarify the rights and responsibilities for both neutrals and belligerents.[12] According to these laws, neutral states must neither assist any of the belligerent parties nor allow their subjects to do so. Those citizens of neutral states who decide to aid one of the belligerents cannot rely on the protection of their state. In fact, such individuals might be punished according to the domestic laws of their own countries. Belligerent states, on the other hand, are expected to respect the commercial and economic activities of neutral parties. Attacks by any of the belligerent parties on neutral shipping often signal the end of neutrality, at least as far as that particular belligerent is concerned.

Contrary to the system of domestic laws, in international law there is no internationally recognized authority to comprehensively enforce the laws of neutrality. Thus, the observance of the rights and responsibilities of neutral states has mainly depended upon the national interests and power bases of belligerent as well as neutral parties in any specific conflict, especially when some or all of the belligerents are among Great Powers. The influence of the concept of power suggests that neutrality has a political as well as legal basis. Some states, like Switzerland, have employed a policy of nonparticipation in any war between other states. This policy, known as permanent neutrality,[13] will be compared with non-alignment later.

In the field of political science, the term *neutrality* often refers to a foreign policy strategy that aims at using the laws of neutrality in case of a war. During peacetime, the foreign policy of a neutral state must meet some unwritten rules, of which the most important is not joining any military, security, or political alliance with any of the potential belligerent states. Generally speaking, a neutral state must avoid making any commitment to potential belligerents that might endanger its neutral stance in case of a war between potential belligerents.[14]

While the Law of Neutrality requires specific measures for a neutral state, a policy of neutrality includes basically voluntary steps taken according to the discretion of the neutral state.[15] All neutral states have a common legal basis for their neutrality according to the Fifth Hague Convention. Their neutrality policies, however, vary because the formulation of such policies depends on diverse geopolitical factors and international conditions.[16]

AN ANALYTICAL DEFINITION OF NON-ALIGNMENT

Grammatically, according to Webster's, the term *non-alignment* is a noun from the adjective "non-aligned" which means "not allied with other nations and especially with one of the Great Powers."[17] This definition could be misinterpreted as using alliance and alignment synonymously. An alliance, however, has a legal basis, binding on the parties to the agreement, whereas an alignment is a general and informal association. Thus, alignment and alliance are not interchangeable terms.[18]

These technical definitions suggest that non-alignment is a situation in which one state refrains from joining any pact with other states and practices a policy of avoiding a formal commitment toward other states. In practice, the strict construction of this definition of non-alignment cannot even be applied to NAM states because they have a commitment to each other.[19] Non-alignment does not mean a lack of commitment to anyone, but rather noncommitment to the superpowers.[20] In sum, non-alignment is briefly defined as the noncommitment of a developing country to one Great Power against another.[21]

Non-Alignment and Permanent Neutrality

Theoretically, the main difference between policies of permanent neutrality and non-alignment lies in the division of the world on the North–South axis. Most LDCs prefer to be called non-aligned rather than neutral, and the majority of neutral states come from developed countries, especially from Europe.[22]

Also, students of non-alignment differentiate non-alignment from permanent neutrality by the nature and function of the policy. From this perspective, many advocates of non-alignment have suggested that non-alignment is a dynamic, fair, and productive policy, while permanent neutrality is timid, static, and isolationist.[23] They consider permanent neutrality as a passive act of nonparticipation not only in conflicts between states, but also in global affairs. For supporters of non-alignment, the passive characteristic of a permanent neutral state is best represented by Switzerland, which has never been a member of the United Nations. This is, however, not to deny the utility of Switzerland, whose strict neutrality policy serves particular diplomatic and financial needs during a crisis.

Non-alignment, on the other hand, is an active policy that promotes a world in which weaker states can live without the intervention of the more powerful states. To protect the weak, NAM states often rely on the pressure of their collective actions and on international public opinion, as in the case of the Dutch attempt to reassert its colonial control of Indonesia following the Japanese surrender in 1945.[24] In other words, non-alignment is a strategy that aims to change the international environment.

Non-alignment suits the needs of many different ideologies, especially those of revolutionary states. Most examples of permanent neutrality share a common European heritage. In this respect, the Marxist ideology of the Eastern bloc countries is an example of an ideology that viewed the world in absolute terms of good and evil and did not respect a neutral position. Thus, the former socialist Yugoslavia had to leave the Second World to be able to take a neutral position in the rivalry between the East and the West. Examples of non-alignment represent diverse non-European traditions, which come from different ideological, socioeconomic, and political backgrounds.[25] Non-alignment is a strategy flexible enough to meet the requirements of the socialist industrialization style of Algeria and the state capitalism of Morocco.

An emphasis on a conspiracy against developing nations is another aspect of non-alignment. Some statesmen of non-aligned countries, particularly revolutionary ones, are convinced that most of the problems they face—like poverty, underdevelopment, colonization, racism, the arms race, and the military and economic hegemony of the major powers—are not isolated but interrelated factors. Revolutionary statesmen believe that these problems undermine the natural development of the weaker states and tend to keep them under the influence of the major powers.[26]

This type of approach implies that many small powers are suspicious of the intentions of more powerful ones. There are three reasons for such suspicion. First, inconsistencies exist between the rhetoric and the actions of Great Powers concerning basic values. For example, the United States maintains that it upholds human rights worldwide, yet, it has assisted regimes that have some of the worst human rights records in the developing world. One can also find inconsistencies between the promises and the practices of the Soviets, as they have supported only those national liberation movements whose activity has a particular strategic value to them. At the same time, they claim to support all anti-imperialistic movements.

Second, strong states maintain that they stand behind international law and institutions, but they also tend to violate the laws or abandon the institutions or their promises to participate fully in them, especially when it does not suit their self-defined national interest. For example, the United States left UNESCO during the Reagan years. Also, the Soviet Union boycotted the Security Council before the Korean War.

Finally, from a North–South perspective, the developing world has historically witnessed that many developed countries tend to have similar economic goals in practice when they interact with lesser developed countries, which are the producers of primary commodities and raw materials. For instance, Revolutionary Iran faced difficult negotiations with the Soviets on setting a fair value for Iranian natural gas. These negotiations broke down several times due to major disagreements between the two parties. The intensity of such negotiations resembled the Anglo–Iranian oil negotiations during the Mossadegh years.[27]

Thus, it seems logical that the practitioners of non-alignment aim to change the world order, which they see as unjust.[28] Revolutionary states are particularly known for taking this approach toward world order, especially during the infancy period of the regime. To change the unjust world, non-aligned countries have set an ambitious international agenda. Regarding economic concerns, these states have asked for the New International Economic Order (NIEO) in order to alter the structure of international economic relations to improve their own terms of trade.[29] On global security issues, NAM supports arms control and disarmament initiatives that aim at the Great Powers, whose military rivalry tends to involve the developing countries.[30]

These demands for a new international order seem to place the supporters of non-alignment among those who have plans for a different world and those who want to change the world immediately and radically.[31] Many followers of non-alignment, contrary to those of neutrality, share the goals of revolutionary idealistic leaders. Since different non-aligned states pursue different non-aligned strategies, the question is raised—are there criteria for identifying non-aligned countries?

Non-Alignment Criteria

The Non-Alignment Movement is the largest gathering of developing countries outside the United Nations. The non-aligned countries, however, are not a homogeneous group. Based on their approaches to foreign policy, there are revolutionary, moderate, and conservative states. For example, Cuba and Vietnam are often among the supporters of the most radical non-alignment approach toward change in the international community.[32] Saudi Arabia and Singapore are among the conservatives, while India and Algeria count as moderate states.[33] Some students of international politics, however, have questioned whether revolutionary states (e.g., Cuba) and conservative states (e.g., Saudi Arabia) are genuinely non-aligned. This raises the questions: Who is really non-aligned and what are the essential criteria for non-alignment?[34] In order to answer such questions, we need to set standards in order to evaluate the various non-alignment strategies.

The first set of criteria for non-alignment is the eligibility criteria for membership in NAM. The basic questions are: Who can join? What is the criteria for membership? What are the basic characteristics of the non-aligned countries? The original membership criteria were provided by the 1961 Preparatory Conference in Cairo and are still in force. I will use the criteria to evaluate the accuracy and extent of the non-alignment commitment of the three revolutionary states under examination:

1. The country concerned should have an independent policy based on the co-existence of states with different political and social systems and based on non-alignment or should be showing a trend in favor of such a policy.

2. It should be consistently supporting movements for national independence.

3. It should not be a member of a multilateral military alliance concluded in the context of Great Power conflict.

4. If it has a bilateral military agreement with a Great Power or is a member of a regional defense pact, the agreement or pact should not be one deliberately concluded in the context of Great Power conflicts.

5. If it has conceded military bases to a foreign power, the concession should not have been made in the context of Great Power conflicts.[35]

The above criteria seek to support five major principles of non-alignment on which the non-aligned countries, revolutionary regimes in particular, base their policies and activities. Any state claiming to follow NAM must be committed to world peace and disarmament, independence, economic equality, cultural identity, universalism, and internationalization.[36] A brief explanation of the background of these principles is in order.

At the time that the movement started, non-aligned countries were concerned with the increasing tension between the two superpowers. Their rivalry tended to involve smaller or weaker nations in their ideological conflict. The founders of the Movement, particularly Jawaharlal Nehru and Marshal Tito, feared a major military confrontation between the two superpowers.

According to NAM, a reduction in international tension requires a nuclear arms control treaty between the Great Powers. In fact, non-alignment literature calls for disarmament and not arms control, and focuses on the nuclear arsenal of the major powers.[37] This does not mean that all non-aligned states accept restrictions on their own sovereign right to develop nuclear technology, especially for peaceful purposes.[38] All NAM conferences, however, have included discussions of great concern over the possibility of a nuclear war.[39]

One can argue that the nuclear capacity of the superpowers also has a psychological influence on revolutionary regimes and contributes not only to their fear of global destruction, but also to their sense of vulnerability. The Non-Alignment Movement has had little direct influence on initiating an arms control treaty between the Great Powers which make their arms decisions independently.[40] The non-aligned states, particularly the revolutionary ones, should receive credit for presenting the international community's concern over a nuclear war by addressing the disarmament issue regularly at their meetings. Additionally, non-alignment as a general strategy has sought to limit the zone of conflict between the two ideological camps and thus has contributed to peace.[41]

This emphasis on peace and disarmament does not mean that a non-aligned state will not declare war on other states or will not become a party to a regional arms race.[42] In the last thirty-five years of NAM history, there have been many military confrontations among the non-aligned countries themselves, many of which involved revolutionary regimes. Examples include the Ethiopia–Somalia War, the Libya–Chad War, and the Iran–Iraq War.[43] The Non-Alignment Movement has not succeeded in settling all such military conflicts, but non-alignment has provided the political base for Algeria's success in defusing the Iranian hostage crisis and settling a diplomatic dispute between a member state and a Great Power. Thus, the record of utilizing non-alignment as a foreign policy strategy has had mixed results.

Independence

The concept of independence is associated with such other concepts as sovereignty and political/legal equality. From this perspective, non-alignment is about independence. After all, NAM was the result of the efforts of the new states of Africa and Asia to conduct a foreign policy independently of, but not isolated from, those of the major powers.[44] The non-aligned states, particularly revolutionary ones, have succeeded in increasing the level of international awareness that foreign policy options are not limited to choosing either the East or the West.

With the term *independence*, non-aligned countries refer to political independence and to the right of all colonial nations to form their own governments.[45] Although the concept of national self-determination did not originate with non-aligned countries, independence has special value for NAM states, particularly revolutionary states that have often gained it by a bloody struggle. Recognizing this special significance, Moscow sought to bring NAM closer to its ideological camp by advocating that they both struggle against Western imperialism.[46] Although NAM's rhetoric has traditionally seemed more anti-Western/American than anti-Eastern/Russian, many non-aligned states have avoided close ties with Moscow, with the exception of Revolutionary Cuba, particularly after the 1979 Havana Conference.[47] Havana–Moscow relations will be analyzed further in Chapter 4.

The concept of independence has different dimensions and cannot be limited to its political form, which is always the first demand of any national liberation movement. After achieving political independence, states often begin to focus on other forms of independence (e.g., economic and cultural) because political independence does not usually alter economic and cultural ties to former colonial powers. This discussion of independence presents a strong argument that the principles of political independence, economic equality, and cultural identity are interrelated. Cultural independence for revolutionary states is as important, if not more so, as economic and political autonomy. The best example in this regard is the emphasis that Revolutionary Iran is placing on cultural independence and its struggle against the influence of foreign cultural values.[48]

Economic Equality

Non-aligned states constitute the majority of the LDCs, and economic development is logically high on their lists of national priorities. Most leaders of NAM, especially those of revolutionary regimes, view the international economic structure as an obstacle to their economic plans. They maintain that the international economic system is highly skewed to the advantage of the Northern countries and have initiated North–South negotiations. As the main target of these negotiations, Western countries have resisted pressure by the South to make economic concessions, and the Soviets have rejected the North–South format for ideological reasons.[49] Through North–South negotiations, non-aligned states have asked for changes to the international economic system in the spirit of NIEO.[50]

Non-aligned states seek to achieve global economic equality by narrowing the gap between rich and poor nations. Revolutionary states often go a step further by aiming to narrow the gap between rich and poor within their own nations as well. The goals of NAM and revolutionary states have been easier said than done. Certainly any international redistribution of wealth requires a major adjustment in Western economic policies. Nevertheless, the West has had little incentive to make any major changes in the current structure of the international economy that has been advantageous for them. That is in part why NAM as a whole, and revolutionary regimes in particular, have not gained meaningful concessions from developed countries. This is the case even though some states have achieved certain economic advantages in their bilateral negotiations with the Northern countries. For instance, Revolutionary China has traditionally given higher priority to economic development than it has to political development. China has attempted to make itself invaluable to Western markets in terms of trade, and this strategy has provided Beijing with the opportunity to gain some advantages. The best example is that the United States values China's trade so highly that Washington renews the most favored nation (MFN) status every year despite its reservations about China's human rights record.

Third World countries, especially those that have strategic significance, have historically gained some economic concessions from the two ideological blocs on foreign aid and trade. By defining many of their domestic problems in terms of East–West issues,[51] some developing countries have succeeded in securing various quantities of economic and technical assistance from one or both superpowers.[52] In the post–Cold War era, prominent developing countries have also been able to secure foreign assistance, investment, and trade from the Great Powers, which are often economic, not ideological, rivals.

On the other hand, some Third World countries have traditionally tried to avoid a definition of their trade disputes with any major power in terms of an East–West issue. This is perhaps a lesson learned from the Anglo–Iranian oil negotiations during the premiership of Mossadegh, from 1951 to 1953. The definition of the oil dispute in East–West terms eventually led to the failure of the negotiations and the Anglo–American support for the 1953 coup against the government of Mossadegh. On trade issues, the major achievement of some LDCs took place in the early 1970s when some members of the Organization of the Petroleum Exporting Countries (OPEC) were able to raise the price of their oil.[53] The oil price hike occurred after some OPEC states gained control of their domestic oil industries from major Western oil companies. Generally speaking, similar attempts by non-aligned producers of raw materials have promoted a one-sided image of non-alignment as an anti-Western strategy. This anti-Western bias of non-alignment regarding oil trade, however, must be put in the context of global economic relations. The West is the predominant consumer of Third World raw materials and commodities. Since disputes naturally occur between the buyers and sellers, one must not categorize all South–West economic disputes in terms of an East–West rivalry. If the East had as significant economic relations with the South as the West, then during economic disputes, the non-alignment strategy of the South would seem to be as anti-Eastern as it does anti-Western. For example, the Iran–Soviet Union natural gas negotiations during the 1980s illustrated that trade with the East is also not carefree.

Cultural Identity

In conjunction with political independence and economic equality, non-aligned countries, especially revolutionary regimes, have sought to protect the cultural identity of their nations. Historically, their cultural identities have suffered setbacks due to cultural pillage undertaken by the Great Powers.[54] To remedy this, some revolutionary regimes attempted to regain whenever possible their national artifacts from foreign museums throughout the world. The task of most revolutionary leaders, however, has been to create a revolutionary citizen who possesses a combination of indigenous characteristics and certain new values.

In recent decades, there is a new and more complex dimension to calls for cultural identity by revolutionary regimes. It involves the telecommunications revolution and the power of the international media. Many leaders of NAM assert that international news agencies, which are mostly Western, not only disseminate news and information, but also Western sociopolitical values, judgments, and traditions.[55]

Third World states established radio and television stations mainly to promote national identity and unity. Many revolutionary leaders, however, argue that these stations indirectly promote alien cultures by broadcasting foreign programs.[56] Consequently, this creates a "cultural duality" between citizens who maintain their indigenous values and traditions and those who adopt foreign values and customs.[57] The reason that networks in the developing world have become dependent upon foreign films and news sources is that they are often a cheaper substitute for more expensive domestic productions.

In response to this situation, most non-aligned countries, particularly revolutionary ones, endorse a new world information and communication order, just as they have supported the New International Economic Order. In practice, this new order has meant linking radio communications among developing countries. Such developments have decreased their dependence for the news and programs on sources from developed countries with all types of ideological persuasions. In addition, domestic film production in many developing countries has increased, despite numerous difficulties. Thus, non-alignment, like a typical revolutionary philosophy, requires the practice of greater selectivity in choosing foreign programs for domestic consumption.[58]

Universalism and Internationalization

The four principles above indicate that non-alignment is a strategy by which a weaker state seeks to protect its national identity and independence in a world ruled by stronger states. Non-alignment strategy, however, has an international aspect—a belief in universalism and internationalization. The latter refers to the efforts of small powers to dominate the agenda of many international meetings, conferences, and organizations with their common economic, political, and social concerns and problems. Revolutionary states are particularly involved in this effort. In fact, one can argue that their foreign policies have succeeded in internationalizing many aspects of their domestic agenda.[59] This style of conducting foreign policy by smaller states is unprecedented in the history of the modern state system.

The most pronounced symbol of commitment by non-aligned states, but not all revolutionary regimes, to universalism is their strong support for the United

Nations system.[60] They are traditionally committed to the U.N. cause, despite the difficulties that veto power and weighted voting practices by the Great Powers have created.[61] Non-aligned states are generally committed to universalism in conducting diplomacy. This has meant a preference for multilateral relations that tend to empower smaller states in dealing with Great Powers. Furthermore, many LDCs opt for internationalization of local problems that they consider too large to be handled in a national or even regional context.[62]

There are three reasons for general support of the United Nations. First, NAM and the United Nations have similar universal goals, particularly regarding the protection of weaker states from aggressive stronger states. Second, the United Nations has served as the main meeting place for smaller states outside the structure of NAM. In fact, non-aligned states have conducted a great deal of their day-to-day activities and functions through their regular ambassadorial meetings at the United Nations. Third, the U.N. is where small powers can express their views on global issues to an international audience which includes Great Powers.

In fact, since the U.N. system has well served most of the developing countries, particularly many non-aligned ones, the latter has not attempted to establish an international organization that might compete with the United Nations. Also, it is interesting to note that NAM has changed both the composition of the United Nations from mainly European to mainly non-European and the focus of the organization from conflict resolution to economic development, particularly since the 1960s.[63] Additionally, non-aligned countries, led by the demands of revolutionary regimes, have succeeded in coordinating their actions within the U.N. system and have formed a rather formidable voting bloc in the General Assembly. In this way, all Great Powers have to lobby their representatives. Therefore, through non-alignment one could argue that the developing world has been able to democratize the public policymaking process at the international level, especially within the U.N. system.[64]

This is not to suggest, however, that the U.N. system is dominated by non-aligned countries. The Security Council certainly illustrates the power of the major states, and this is symbolized by their permanent membership and veto rights. Even in the U.N. General Assembly, where developing countries constitute the majority, Great Powers are not powerless to pass their resolutions. Finally, Western developed countries have a highly visible role and presence in major international institutions, like the World Bank and the International Monetary Fund, where their economic might translates into undeniable political power.

APPROACHES TO NON-ALIGNMENT

As indicated earlier, this chapter does not entail a discussion of major non-alignment theories. I will, however, introduce two major non-alignment approaches to foreign policy, which I refer to as a point of reference in analyzing the foreign relations of revolutionary China, Cuba, and Iran.

Equidistance and natural allies approaches explain the foreign policy strategy of developing states since the early days of NAM. By applying these approaches to the three case studies, we can begin to understand to what degree they explain the foreign relations of each revolutionary state and examine the shortcomings of each approach.

The supporters of the natural allies approach argue that the developing world and the Soviet bloc are natural allies in their struggle against Western imperialism.[65] Angola, Cuba, Ethiopia, and Vietnam have been among the supporters of the natural allies approach.

Cuba advocates the natural allies approach because of the anti-imperialistic nature of non-alignment and its support for national liberation movements. The Cuban leaders reject the equidistance approach on the grounds that this approach treats friend and foe alike. Havana has historically disapproved of the equal treatment of superpowers for ideological reasons.

On the other hand, the supporters of equidistance have traditionally considered both superpowers as expansionist states. Using this approach, a smaller state does not need to isolate itself from superpowers but must try to maintain equal relations with them.[66] The supporters of this approach come from diverse backgrounds. Some, like the former Yugoslavia, were socialist states while others, like Singapore, are closely associated with the Western world. Still others, like India, have taken a unique approach in their foreign policies.[67]

NOTES

1. Leo Mates, *Non-Alignment: Theory and Current Policy* (Belgrade: Oceana Publication, 1972).

2. M. S. Rajan, "The Concept of Non-Alignment and the Basis of Membership in the Movement," in K. P. Misra and K. R. Narayanan, eds. *Non-Alignment in Contemporary International Relations* (New Delhi: Vikas Publishing, 1981).

3. William C. Johnstone, *Foreign Policy: A Study in Neutralism* (Cambridge: Harvard University Press, 1963).

4. Mates, 80-81.

5. Alastair Buchan, "Bipolarity and Coalition," *Pacific Community* 5, no. 3 (April 1974): 348-62.

6. For a survey of different approaches toward the Cold War, see Walter LaFeber, *America, Russia, and the Cold War, 1945–1990*, 6th ed. (New York: McGraw-Hill, 1991). Also see Kenneth W. Thompson, *World Polarization, 1943–1953*, vol. 1 of *Cold War Theories* (Baton Rouge: Louisiana State University Press, 1981).

7. For more details on the origin of non-alignment see Edvard Kardelj, "Historical Roots of Non-Alignment," *Bulletin of Peace Proposals* 7, no. 1 (1976): 84-89; Harry Sichrousky, "Non-Alignment: Basis, History, and Prospects," *Afro-Asian and World Affairs*, 2, no. 1 (Spring 1965): 19-27; Peter Willets, *The Non-Aligned Movement: The Origins of a Third World Alliance* (Bombay, India: Popular Prakashan, 1978).

8. Webster's New Collegiate Dictionary (Springfield, Mass.: G. and C. Merriam, 1973).

9. On the concept of neutrality in Europe, see K. E. Birnbaum and H. P. Neuhold, eds., *Neutrality and Non-Alignment in Europe* (Vienna: Braumuller, 1981).

10. H. Blix, *Sovereignty, Aggression, and Neutrality* (Stockholm, Sweden: Almqvis and Wiksell, 1970).

11. Daniel Frei, "Neutrality," in *World Encyclopedia of Peace*, ed. Linus Pauling (Oxford: Pergamon Press, 1986).

12. Gerhard Von Glahn, *Law Among Nations*, 3rd ed. (New York: MacMillan, 1976), 621-61.

13. For an analysis of permanent neutrality, see H. P. Neuhold, "Permanent Neutrality in Contemporary International Relations," *Irish Studies International Affairs* 1, no. 3 (1982): 13-26.

14. Daniel Frei, "Neutrality and Non-Alignment," *Korea and World Affairs* 3, no. 3 (1971): 275-86.

15. R. Ogley, *The Theory and Practice of Neutrality in the Twentieth Century* (London: Routledge and Kegan Paul, 1970).

16. Frei, 30.

17. *Webster's New Collegiate Dictionary*, 780. The dictionary uses the term *nations*, but it should be *states*.

18. Ibid., 30.

19. Bozica Blagovic, "The Ideological and Political Foundations of Non-Alignment," *Review of International Affairs* 32, nos. 752-53 (5-20 August 1981): 5-8; P. V. Rao Narasimha, "Adherence to the Principles and Aims of Non-Alignment," *Review of International Affairs* 31, no. 724 (5 June 1980): 1-6.

20. Attributable to Professor Inis L. Claude, University of Virginia, 1992.

21. O. Jankowitsch and K. P. Sauvant, eds., *The Third World Without Superpowers: The Collected Documents of the Non-Aligned Countries* (New York: Oceana, 1978); Leo Mates, "Non-Alignment and the Great Powers," *Foreign Affairs* (1970): 526-36.

22. H. Hakovirta, "The Soviet Union and the Varieties of Neutrality in Europe," *World Politics* 35, no. 4 (1983): 563-85; M. Jakobson, *Finnish Neutrality* (London: 1968); P. Keating, *A Singular Stance: Irish Neutrality in the 1980's* (Dublin: 1984.)

23. The following sources provide the academic background for the characterization of non-alignment: B. Kirthisinghe, "Non-Alignment Is Not Neutralism," *Modern Review* 123, no. 4 (April 1968): 235-38; K. P. Misra, "Non-Alignment: A Dynamic Concept," Indian and Foreign Review 12, no. 21 (15 August 1975): 11-12; M. Nikezic, "Why Uncommitted Countries Hold That They Are Non Neutral," *Annals of the American Academy of Political and Social Science*, 336 (July 1961): 75-82; M. Petkovic, "Non-Alignment and Neutrality," *Review of International Affairs* 17, no. 400 (5 December 1966):1-2; B. Tadic, "Non-Alignment and Neutrality in the Contemporary World," *Review of International Affairs* 653 (5 June 1977): 11-12.

24. Krishan Gopal, *Non-Alignment and Power Politics* (New Delhi: V. I. Publications, 1983).

25. K. P. Misra, "Ideological Bases of Non-Alignment," in *The Principles of Non-Alignment* ed. H. Kochler (London: Third World Press, 1982).

26. Linus Pauling, ed., *World Encyclopedia of Peace*, (Oxford: Pergamon Press, 1986), 60.

27. Helen Metz, ed., *Iran: A Country Study* (Washington D.C.: U.S. Government Printing Office, 1989), 162.

28. Y. Jan, "We Support the Just Struggle of the Non-Aligned Countries," *Review of International Affairs* 30, no. 692 (5 February 1979): 4-6.

29. Nitin Desai, "Non-alignment and the New International Economic Order," in ed. U. S. Bajpai, *Non-Alignment: Perspectives and Prospects* (New Delhi: Lancers Publishers, 1983), 174-200. Also see Samir Amin, "After the New International Economic Order: The Future of International Economic Relations," in Bajpai, 201-17.

30. P. R. Chari, "Non-alignment and Disarmament," in Bajpai, 117-131.

31. K. D. Gyu, "Non-Alignment: A Revolutionary Force," *Review of International Affairs* 27, no. 620 (5 February 1976): 1-3.

32. K. P. Karunakaran, "Non-aligned Radicals," *Seminar* 45 (May 1963): 17-22.

33. D. Belovski, "The Activities and Aims of Yugoslavia as a Non-Aligned and Socialist Country," *Review of International Affairs* 21 no. 480, (1970): 3-6; and I. Malhotra, "Non-Alignment: the Indian Approach," *Indian Calling* (July 1976): 2-3.

34. M. S. Rajan, "The Concept of Non-Alignment and the Basis of Membership in the Movement," Paper Presented at the Indo–Yugoslav Symposium on Non-Alignment, 14-17 May 1980 (New Delhi: Jawaharlal Nehru University, 1980); "Who Are Non-Aligned?" *Economic and Political Weekly* 3, no. 16 (20 April 1968): 627-28.

35. N. Krishnan, "Non-alignment–Movement or Organization?," in Misra and Narayanan, 255-56.

36. A. W. Singham and Shirley Hune, *Non-Alignment in an Age of Alignments* (London: Zed Books, 1986), 15-32.

37. A. S. Lall, "The Non-Aligned in the Disarmament Negotiations," *Bulletin of the Atomic Scientists* 20, no. 5 (May 1964): 17-21.

38. E. Kiljun, "Non-Aligned Countries and Peaceful Uses of Nuclear Power," *Review of International Affairs* 28, no. 686 (5 November 1978): 10-12.

39. For example, see B. Brankovic, "The Sixth Conference and Disarmament," *Review of International Affairs* 30, no. 710 (5 November 1979): 7-10; H. Jack, "A Disarmament and the Algiers Summit," *Review of International Affairs* 24, no. 551 (20 March 1973): 6-10.

40. On the American and Soviet traditional relations regarding arms control initiatives, see Alva Myrdal, *The Game of Disarmament: How the United States and Russia Run the Arms Race* (New York: Pantheon Books, 1976).

41. P. K. Jha, "The Role of Non-Aligned Powers in the Eighteen Nation Disarmament Committee," *Afro–Asia and World Affairs* 5, no. 1 (Spring 1968): 57-66.

42. For data on military capability, see SIPRI, *Yearbook of World Armament and Disarmament* (London: Taylor and Francis, 1982). Some NAM states have developed a domestic arms industry of their own, see "China in Nuclear Forces Build up," *Jane's Defense Weekly* (15 April 1989): 642; V. Harle, "The Development of Arms Technology and Small Countries," *Yearbook of Finnish Foreign Policy 1980* (Helsinki: Finnish Institute of International Affairs, 1981): 2-11; J. Bruce, "Iran Building up Its Own Arms Industry," *Jane's Defense Weekly* 20 (June 1987): 1302; S. Zaloga, "Ballistic Missiles in the Third World," *International Defense Review* (November 1988): 1423-27.

43. D. Mujezinovic, "The War Between Iraq and Iran: The VII Conference of Non-Aligned Countries in Baghdad," *Review of International Affairs* 33, no. 76 (5 February 1982): 1-5.

44. C. P. Bhambhri, "Assertion of Independence," *Secular Democracy* 9 nos. 14-15 (31 July and 15 August 1976): 103-107; M. Komatina, Non-Aligned: The Independence Revolution," *Review of International Affairs* (5 January 1977): 14-16 and 19-30; S. Mukherjee, "Independence and Non-Alignment," *New-Age* (15 August 1976): 11-12; K. P.

Narayanan, "Non-Alignment, Independence, and National Interest," paper presented at the Indo–Yugoslav Symposium on Non-Alignment, 14-17 May 1980, (New Delhi: Jawaharlal Nehru University, 1980).

45. "Non-Aligned Extend Support to African Struggle for Liberation," *Times of India*, 12 April 1977, 1-3; Z. Rosales, "Role of the Movement of Non-Aligned Countries in the Struggle of the Peoples for National Independence and World Peace," paper presented at the International Conference on Principles of Non-Alignment, 4-6 May 1982 (Baghdad: Government Printing House).

46. R. Ulyanovsky, "Non-Alignment Movement and Anti-Imperialist Struggle," *Soviet Review* 16, no. 39 (27 August 1979): 9-11.

47. R. Allison, *The Soviet Union and the Strategy of Non-Alignment in the Third World* (Cambridge: Cambridge University Press, 1988), 242-52.

48. Peter Waldman, "Iran Fights New Foe: Western Television," *The Wall Street Journal*, (8 August 1994).

49. Allison, 34.

50. K. P. Sauvant and O. Jankowitsch, "The Initiating Role of the Non-Aligned Countries, "*Changing Priorities on the International Agenda: The New International Economic Order* in ed. K. P. Sauvant (New York: Pergamon, 1981).

51. On the economic difficulties of less developed countries, see Gunnar Myrdal, *Asian Drama: An Inquiry into the Poverty of Nations* (Harmondsworth, N.Y.: Penguin, 1968).

52. For a review of U.S. aid to the non-aligned countries, see Agency for International Development, *U.S. Overseas Loans and Grants* (Washington, D.C.: U.S. Government Printing Office, 1990). For a review of Soviet aid to the non-aligned countries, see U.S. Department of State, *Soviet and East European Aid to the Third World, 1981* (Washington, D.C.: U.S. Government Printing Office, 1983).

53. For an analysis of OPEC's record, see G. Williams, *Third-World Political Organizations* (Montclair, N. J.: Allanheld, Osmun, 1981), 79-90.

54. Singham and Hune, 25.

55. H. I. Schiller, "Mechanisms of Cultural Imperialism," *The Non-Aligned Movement in World Politics* in ed. A. W. Singham (Westport, Conn.: Lawrence Hill, 1977).

56. Waldman.

57. On the impact of the media in the Third World, see P. Ivacic, "Decolonization of Information," *Socialist Thought and Practice* 16, no. 9 (1976); D.R. Mankekar, *One Way Free Flow: Neo-Colonialism Via News Media* (New Delhi: Clarion Books, 1978); W. Pisarek, "Communication Explosion and the Third World," *Communication* 10 no. 10 (1975): 21-23; H. Schiller, "Genesis of the Free Flow of Information Principles: The Imposition of Communication Domination," *Democratic Journalist* , (1977): 7-12.

58. B. Bogonovic, "Non-Aligned Information Media to Strengthen Cooperation," *Review of International Affairs* 27 (5 March 1976): 25-27; "Boost for U.N. Non-Aligned News Pool Ties," *Hindustan Times* 59 no. 303 (4 November, 1982): 24-25; D. R. Mankekar, "Newspool: A Corrective to Western News Agencies," *Organizer* (15 August 1979); G. R. Naesselond, "Introduction to a New Information Order," *Democratic Journalist* 4 (1977): 3-6; B. Pavuc, "Transnational Companies and Communication Among the Non-Aligned," *Review of International Affairs* 27 (February 1976): 14-17; H. Topul, "Disequilibrium of Information," *Media Asia* (Singapore) 3, no. 3 (1976); C. Vockovic, "Equality and the News and Information Monopoly," *Review of International Affairs* 32, no. 760 (5 December 1981): 25-27.

59. J. Vrhovec, "Non-Alignment: A Universal Policy," *Review of International Affairs* 30, no. 694 (5 March 1979): 1-4.

60. A. Bakocevic, "Non-Alignment and the United Nations," *Review of International Affairs* 30, no. 711 (20 November 1979): 10-12; K. P. Saksena, "Non-Alignment and the United Nations," *International Studies* 20, nos. 1-2 (January-June 1981): 81-101.

61. On the veto problem in the United Nations, see Inis L. Claude, Jr., *Swords into Plowshares*, 4th ed. (New York: Random House, 1984), 141-162.

62. On the implications of collective international actions, see Inis. L. Claude, Jr., "Collective Legitimization as a Political Function of the United Nations," *International Organization: Politics and Process* in eds. L. M. Goodrich and D. A. Kay (Madison: University of Wisconsin Press, 1973), 209-221.

63. T. Hovet, Jr., *Bloc Politics in the United Nations* (Cambridge: Harvard University Press, 1960).

64. A. M. Grobe-Jutte, "From Hierarchial to Egalitarian International Decision Structure: Non-Aligned Policies in the U.N. System," *Future Prospects of International Organization* in ed. R. Jutte (London: Frances Printer, 1981); C. Job, "Democratic Character of the Non-Aligned Movement: After the Sixth Summit," *Review of International Affairs* 30, no. 712 (5 December 1979): 28-30; M. Komatina, "Democratization of International Relations: A Programmatic Postulate of the Non-Aligned Countries," *Review of International Affairs* 29, no. 671 (20 March 1978): 27-29; S. Nick, "Action Forms in the Non-Aligned Movement and Advancement of Democratic Relations Within its Framework," *Review of International Affairs* 32, no. 761 (20 December, 1981): 8-11.

65. "USSR Loyal Friend of Non-Alignment Movement," *Soviet Review* 13, no. 39 (28 August 1976): 2-4; "USSR as Non-Aligned Nations' Natural Ally," *Current Digest of the Soviet Press* 28, no. 32 (8 September 1976): 11-13.

66. N. P. Nayar, "Middle Ground Between Russia and America: an Indian View," *Foreign Affairs* (31 January 1954): 259-69; R. Petkovic, "Non-Alignment and the Equidistance Theory," *Review of International Affairs* 25, no. 581 (20 June 1974): 8-10.

67. D. C. Pande, *India's Foreign Policy as an Exercise in Non-Alignment* (New Delhi: Devendra Printers, 1988).

3

CHINESE FOREIGN RELATIONS, 1949–1959

In the second half of the twentieth century, Chinese leaders have often surprised foreign observers, especially those focusing on Chinese foreign relations. The literature includes many examples of expert astonishment at political events in the People's Republic of China (PRC).[1] These include the unexpected triumph of the revolutionary Chinese over Chiang Kai-shek's forces in 1949, Revolutionary China's entrance into the Korean War in 1950, The Quemoy Island Crisis in 1958, the 1963 public breakup of Sino–Soviet relations, China's entrance into the nuclear age in 1964, the revival of Sino–American diplomatic ties in 1972, the 1989 massacre in Tiananmen Square, and China's hostile reaction to the unofficial June 1995 visit of the Taiwanese president to the United States. In sum, depending upon one's perspective, China has been a source of either pleasant or unpleasant surprises.

References to China's so-called unexpected or unpredictable policy,[2] however, imply that our understanding of Chinese behavior is far from complete. We need to reassess our knowledge about the formulation and implementation of Chinese foreign policy, particularly from a more balanced perspective. A key issue is our incomplete perception of Chinese behavior, which tends to be "Western-centric." One factor explaining the failure of the United States to respond more appropriately to Chinese affairs is our misperception of Chinese and their behavior.[3] Responding to the need for a more balanced perspective, I explain Chinese foreign relations by considering a Chinese interpretation of events, short of justifying or apologizing for Chinese policy misconduct. Like leaders of other developing countries, the Chinese have made errors in some policy choices. In their rapid drive for modernization, Beijing resorted to some shortcuts, that involved violence as is the case of Tiananmen Square. Obviously, there is no excuse for China's use of force in dealing with political opposition, or in reaching foreign policy goals; yet, this does not mean that one should ignore the Chinese perspective. Thus, an underlying theme of this chapter is a balance between the Chinese and Western world views in analyzing foreign relations of Revolutionary China.[4]

Policymakers, scholars, and ordinary citizens can have a more comprehensive understanding of the Chinese Government's behavior if it is not viewed only from a Western, particularly an American, perspective.[5] This reassessment is especially possible now due to two factors. First, our analytical perception is no longer contaminated with a zero-sum Cold War thinking.[6] The second factor is the availability of new primary and secondary sources. Some government records from the 1949–1959 period in Russia, America, and China have been declassified. Also a few new publications raise questions about some old assumptions regarding the foreign relations of Revolutionary China and the real intentions of its leaders.[7]

The scope of this chapter is limited to the 1949–1959 period, because an extensive analysis of Chinese foreign relations since the 1949 Revolution is suitable for a more comprehensive study. My main purpose is to reexamine our general knowledge of Chinese foreign relations during the first decade following the 1949 Revolution, when the nature and impact of leadership was more significant than those of institutions. Analyzing this crucial period will also aid in better understanding Beijing's present-day foreign policy.

In the literature, the general consensus is that the foreign policy of Revolutionary China from 1949 to 1971 was predominantly conflictual with an isolationist tone. And with the early 1980s, a more conciliatory stance by the People's Republic of China was visible, especially toward the Western states. I argue, however, that the foreign policy posture of Red China cannot be solely categorized as hostile during the entire first decade of the revolution. In fact, one can observe a trend in Chinese foreign relations with three distinct stages: a two-track policy period, a conflictual era, and a more conciliatory period.

ELEMENTS OF CHINESE FOREIGN POLICY

Revolutionary China was a pioneer among the developing countries in pursuing a foreign policy independently of major powers. This occurred long before the Non-Alignment Movement was formally organized in 1961 and before non-alignment strategy was widely recognized as a policy option for many Third World states.

In fact, one should give credit to Revolutionary China for conducting its foreign relations independently, for the most part, from both superpowers since 1949. This course of action was taken long before the Twelfth Party Congress in 1982, when the Chinese Communist Party (CCP) officially adopted its independent foreign policy. The latter, however, was actually in practice from the time of the revolution.

Interestingly enough, Beijing never formally joined NAM, although it explicitly adjusted its foreign policy goals in order to coincide with the five criteria for a non-

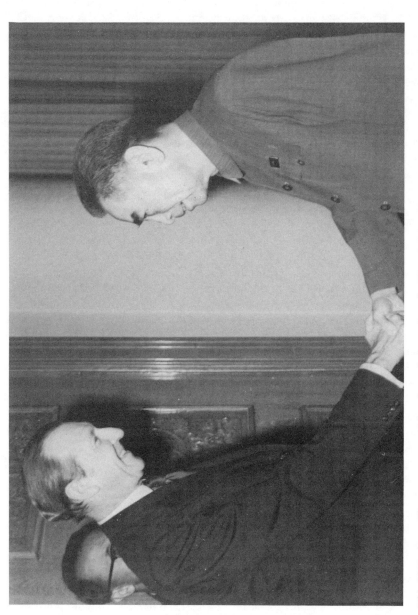

This 1972 picture illustrates a congenial exchange between Premier Zhou Enlai and UN Secretary General Kurt Waldheim, after China's so-called opening to the West. Long before such warm exchanges, however, Beijing had already shown conciliatory gestures toward the West, as early as the first decade following the 1949 Revolution. *Photograph courtesy of UN/DPI Photo.*

alignment strategy. Thus, it is challenging to apply the concept of non-alignment to Revolutionary China mainly because Beijing neither publicly declared such a strategy nor have many Chinese scholars and/or policymakers asserted that the People's Republic of China attempted to pursue such a strategy. This does not, however, mean that China did not adopt a non-aligned posture. In fact, China was a pioneer in utilizing many of the principles associated with such a strategy, and its general policy toward the Third World has served as an indicator of its overall strategy. The latter has theoretically stood on five fundamental notions: Contradictions, United Front, Lean to One Side, Intermediate Zone, and Third International Force.

Contradictions and the Theory of Semi-colonialism

One of Mao's contributions is the well-known theory of semi-colonialism, which is based on the concept of contradictions. He considered contradictions to be the theoretical agent for change in both social and political structures. According to Mao, "The fundamental cause of the development of a thing is not external, but internal; it lies in the contradictoriness within the thing. There is internal contradiction in every single thing, hence its motion and development."[8] Mao used contradictions to refer to his application of the Marxist concept of class struggle to Chinese domestic and international affairs. The main question was the location of these contradictions. In response, one expert stated: "For Mao the contradiction between imperialism and China was the principal contradiction and it therefore overshadowed that between feudalism and the Chinese masses. Put simply, this meant that China's internal affairs were dominated by the outside world."[9]

The significance of the concept contradictions was in the role it played in Mao's theory of semicolonialism. Briefly, the theory referred to China as a semicolony whose territory was controlled by several colonial powers, and Mao theorized that China could protect its independence by successfully maneuvering between rival colonial powers. The crux of this theory dates to the traditional Chinese strategy of "using barbarians to subdue barbarians."[10] But Mao contributed to the theory by combining it with the concept of class struggle. He also presumed an international application for this theory beyond its relevance to the domestic affairs of China.

The semicolonialism theory was based on China's experience with the colonial powers. This experience was different from those of most other African and Asian nations. For example, unlike India, China was being simultaneously exploited by several colonial powers that tried to act in concert and avoid conflict. The rivalry among these powers provided China with an opportunity to benefit from their contradictions. In the mid–1930s, Mao analyzed the positive and negative aspects of the contradictions existing in Chinese affairs and concluded that "the revolution would be victorious, but only by means of a long and flexible struggle, adjusting as required to the changes in the balance and relationships of the opposed forces of imperialism and its political allies in China."[11]

The leadership of Revolutionary China also found the concept of contradiction useful in formulating foreign policy after the 1949 Revolution. Before the revolution, the Chinese leaders, particularly Mao, emphasized the applicability of these ideas in China due to the country's unique circumstances, while after the revolution the basic theoretical notion was "more contradictions mean more struggle and ultimately more revolution."[12]

The Concept of United Front

Associated with the terms contradictions and semi-colonialism was the concept of united front.[13] Three months before the success of the October Revolution, Mao clearly asserted united front as a national and international strategy.[14] This concept was also another legacy of the prerevolutionary era and its value was in dealing with a common enemy,[15] just like the struggle of the non-aligned states with hegemonic powers.[16]

United front as a strategy is not an original invention of revolutionary China and many of its basic ideas date to prerevolutionary Chinese literature[17] and to Lenin's writings.[18] This concept, however, has substantial relevance to the history of Revolutionary China,[19] and Chinese leaders, particularly Mao, have contributed to the theoretical development of this strategy.[20]

In general, the united front concept is defined as "a limited and temporary alignment between a Communist party or state and one or more non-Communist political units with the dual purpose, on the Communist side, of confronting a common enemy and furthering the revolutionary cause."[21] Mao added that the purpose of this strategy was "to make use of contradictions, win over the many, oppose the few, and crush our enemies one by one."[22]

Mao had often advocated that imperialism would intensify the contradictions between the classes in China and would for nationalistic reasons direct more people to the side of the revolutionaries. In the late 1930s, as Japan began its military campaign in China, this outright aggression prepared the Chinese political environment for a national united front against Japan between the CCP and the Kuomintang (KMT), China's nationalist party. Later Mao added that the same method must be used against the other colonial powers. Mao summarized the logic of the strategy as follows:

> When imperialism launches a war of aggression against [a semi-colonial country], all its various classes, except for some traitors, can temporarily unite in a national war against imperialism. At such a time, the contradiction between imperialism and the country concerned becomes the principal contradiction, while all the contradictions among the various classes within the country ... are temporarily relegated to a secondary and subordinate position.[23]

Mao's main argument in linking the concepts of contradictions, semi-colonialism, and united front can be summarized as follows:

In any period of history one "contradiction" (and therefore one enemy) will be more important than the rest; as all other contradictions are secondary to this "principal contradiction," the objective possibility exists of uniting all other forces against the "principal enemy"; the historical role of the Communist Party is to perceive the "principal contradiction" and turn the objective possibility of a united front into a reality; a particular united front is always temporary, for once its purpose is accomplished a new "principal contradiction" will emerge and the process will be repeated.[24]

In sum, Mao aimed at a long-term strategy for promoting world revolution. This strategy was based on the CCP's ideology and experience. It portrayed China as an initiator of, rather than a reactor to, events. The united front strategy reflects the significance of ideology in the foreign policy of Revolutionary China. This is not to say that Chinese policy was solely determined by one variable (i.e., ideology), but to emphasize that this strategy follows the CCP's experience in fighting a revolutionary war at home and promoting revolutionary changes abroad. The application of this concept to Chinese foreign relations was partly because of its earlier success in the domestic arena.

"Lean to One Side" or Alliance

Chinese foreign policy also possessed short-term objectives that were largely shaped by external political realities and were therefore more reactive in nature. Students of international relations who focus on the study of alliances, often discuss this aspect of Chinese foreign policy, emphasizing security threats, which are considered the main variables contributing to the formulation of a specific policy. For example, Allen Whiting argued that China's decision to enter the Korean War was based on Beijing's perception of an external threat.[25] Although approaches based on power alignments do not deny completely the role of ideology, they often discount it to a level that could justify almost any diplomatic initiative that Revolutionary China would have wished to make.[26]

Defining an alliance as a formal military commitment of one state to another in case of an invasion,[27] Beijing signed the Sino-Soviet Treaty of Friendship, Alliance, and Mutual Assistance on 14 February 1950, a month after the Soviets had boycotted the Security Council. From a Western perspective, this treaty and Mao's famous slogan "lean to one side" seemed to suggest that there was no room for an independent and non-aligned position in the foreign affairs of Revolutionary China, at least in the first decade after the revolution. To understand China's real motives, however, these diplomatic moves must be considered within China's national and international context.

One may question a "lean to one side." The answer lies in part in the ideological connection between the People's Republic of China and the Soviet Union and in part in the new international realities facing Revolutionary China at the time. In the early days of the revolution, Mao stated the reasons for "lean to one side" by saying: "The forty years' experience of Sun Yat-sen and the twenty-eight years' experience of the Communist Party have taught us to lean to one side, and we are firmly convinced that in order to win victory and consolidate it we must lean to one side."[28] Mao also portrayed a world divided into two camps and asked the Chinese to decide if they were on the side of imperialism or socialism. He ignored the possibility of any other choices by adding: "Sitting on the fence will not do, nor is there a third road. We oppose the Chiang Kai-shek reactionaries who lean to the side of imperialism, and we also oppose the illusions about a third road."[29]

By taking the side of socialism, Mao did not mean to limit Chinese policy options or to isolate the new regime. Isolation was not accepted because Mao stated that victory was not possible without international assistance. Although he differentiated between the intentions of the East and the West to provide aid, he did not rule out the possibility of ties with the West.[30] In fact, he blamed the reactionaries for hindering China from establishing diplomatic relations with other states that were based on "equality, mutual benefit and mutual respect for territorial integrity and sovereignty."[31] These factors remained the core ideas of his other strategy, namely, Mao's version of non-alignment. These ideas also became a part of the philosophical foundation of the NAM.

Despite Soviet ties to the KMT and the rocky relations between the Chinese Communist Party and the Communist Party of the Soviet Union (CPSU), Mao initially decided to "lean to one side," which surprised some observers.[32] He presumed that an alignment with the Soviet Union would serve both the national and international objectives of the regime. Considering that the United States had already labeled China a Soviet puppet, China did not have much to lose by aligning itself with the Soviet Union.

In domestic affairs, China hoped that this strategy would provide the military backing and political assurance to permit a reduction in the expensive military arena and to allow the task of national construction. Some argued that the Sino–Soviet alliance also had a tactical value, for Mao "used the alliance with Stalin to consolidate his own power."[33] In foreign affairs, the issue was the international position of the People's Republic of China during an acute Cold War. Moreover, the Soviet Union was "the leader of the world communist bloc and therefore the only realistic major ally for a communist China."[34] Notwithstanding the ideological differences between Beijing and Moscow, any Chinese government would have been forced to come to terms with the Soviets, especially to renegotiate the outstanding Soviet–KMT treaty of August 1945.[35]

There has been much speculation about China's objective to "lean to one side, which had other well-known supporters, like Madam Sun Yat-Sen."[36] The evidence leads to three main conclusions: first, it was essential for both strategic and economic reasons;[37] second, it was not necessarily a predetermined move; and finally, it did not come about easily. The last point was clear when in December 1958, Mao testified that the alliance treaty negotiations with Stalin were not easy and that there were many contending issues between the two sides.[38] This treaty was the result of a two-month-long visit to Moscow by Mao, who described the task of the Chinese mission as strengthening relations instead of a "joyous affirmation of proletarian internationalism." There were also other hints that the political environment in general and the negotiations in particular were not as cooperative or constructive as expected.[39] The result was a treaty that fell short of the expectations of the Chinese leaders, but as one expert asserted: "The real value of the Treaty and the alliance which it embodied was ... a strategic one, for it provided China above all with an ally at a time when the new revolutionary state was at its most vulnerable."[40]

According to Article I of the treaty, the parties were to assist each other fully in case of an attack by Japan or any of its allies (namely, the United States.).[41] China's concern with the American threat in East Asia in the early 1950s was contrary to its mid–1940s view of the benign Americans who began to disarm and demobilize soon after World War II and who were fixated on Europe and the Soviet Union.[42] China was willing to pay a political price associated with the alliance as long as it obtained the military protection it assumed it had gained from the Soviets. As one student of Chinese affairs concluded: "As the future course of Sino-Soviet relations would show, once that guarantee became devalued, then the currency of the whole relationship lost its fiduciary backing."[43]

The nature of the Sino–Soviet alliance was different from that of the Warsaw Pact in which the Soviets were obviously in full control. The Russians could not, however, control the Chinese. Since before the revolution, the CCP had advocated equality among communist parties, despite its nominal acceptance of the Soviet leadership of the socialist world. Thus, the term *alignment* may seem more appropriate than alliance for describing ties between Beijing and Moscow.

To better understand the nature of this alignment, we can examine it from the perspective of other approaches covered in this study. For example, contrary to its formal image, "lean to one side" can be viewed in a more temporary and general form as a united front against the immediate threat at the time—the United States. The temporary nature of Chinese alignment with the Soviets makes more sense when one considers the growing contradictions in the Moscow–Beijing relationship, of which many Chinese patriots,[44] as well as Mao himself,[45] were quite aware. The Sino–Soviet alliance can also represent a "convergence of interests" approach.[46] In either case, the People's Republic of China did not completely lose its independence in foreign policymaking.

From another perspective, one can argue that an alignment with Moscow in the early 1950s balanced their open rivalry by the end of the decade. This in itself can be viewed as a sort of non-alignment strategy in the long term.

Intermediate Zone and Third International Force

In 1946 from his Yenan cave, Mao introduced the idea of an intermediate zone, which referred generally to those countries lying between the socialist and capitalist worlds. This concept was often used in the context of small power—Great Power relations, and Mao revived it in 1958.[47] Some scholars have defined this zone, which included China, as "the revolutionary battlefield of the world which lay between the two Great Powers."[48] Mao hypothesized that American imperialism must first take over this zone before it actually challenged the Soviets on their own land.[49] Thus, the zone was the front against imperialism.

Mao's often vague notion of the intermediate zone corresponded to the familiar concept of Third World. The latter he had originally rejected while portraying the international system as a divided world between the two camps of socialism and capitalism with no place for a third "independent" force.[50]

The term *intermediate zone*, however, is significant in the development of the Chinese world view and its foreign policy shift from a "lean to one side" to a more typical non-alignment strategy. In both 1946 and 1958, the emphasis on the concept of zone also showed optimism among Chinese leaders about expanding their policy options[51] despite a tense international setting that would seem rather pessimistic to many students of the Cold War.

Intermediate zone, however, was not a new idea based on Mao's thought (Maoism). In fact, one can relate its strategic and geographic notion to Beijing's Sino-centric view of the world or what some have called the "middle kingdom" approach. This basically meant that political power originated from the core of the Chinese empire, radiated to the peripheral landmass, and declined with distance and accessibility. This perspective suggests a series of peripheral zones (around the center of the Chinese powerhouse), each of which had a particular relationship with the core.[52] The relevance of this idea for the People's Republic of China is best formulated by one expert:

> There is no reason to believe that this cultural, geographic and strategic view of the outside world had altogether disappeared with the advent of China's Communist leadership. The model may be said to have retained considerable relevance for Chinese foreign policy in so far as that policy has to contend with certain inescapable political and geographic realities.[53]

The intermediate zone expanded with time as the general international balance of forces shifted. In the late 1940s, the zone was basically composed of the African, Asian, and Latin American nations that shared with China an anti-colonial and pro-economic development commitment. By the late 1950s and the early 1960s, it also included those industrialized nations of the East (e.g., Romania) and West (e.g., France) that shared Revolutionary China's opposition to the hegemonic ambitions of the superpowers. In January 1964, Sino–French negotiations for establishing full diplomatic relations also became the occasion for the official redefinition of the concept of the intermediate zone. The latter, the Chinese proclaimed consisted of two parts: the African, Asian, and Latin American states that were trying to protect their independence; and Western Europe, which was subject to U.S. control.[54] Later the Chinese included the whole of Europe in the zone and argued that the two superpowers had sandwiched the other countries between themselves.[55] In general, the concept of an intermediate zone did not relate to a specific geographic region. This indicated flexibility in Chinese strategy to isolate her main foes by forming a united front with friendly states sharing a common cause. This also illustrates how the notions of united front and intermediate zone are linked.

The Chinese leaders gradually began to theorize that at least some of the states in the intermediate zone could act like a third force, independently of both superpowers. In the long term, the feasibility of this third force gave more flexibility to the Chinese to act independently of both superpowers in foreign affairs. It also provided opportunities for a more pragmatic and less revolutionary China. For revolutionary realists, "lean to one side" was partly an ideological and partly a pragmatic choice for there was little room for a third force at the height of the Cold War. As the Cold War began to stagnate, however, foreign policy options of the intermediate zone states increased. Thus, Chinese foreign relations with the zone were a function of China's revolutionary ideology as well as the political realities of a world in transition.

By the mid–1950s, the world found a more accommodating and flexible China at the Bandung Conference. Beijing's more confident posture and increasingly independent (from Moscow) foreign policy line ironically led to a more radical non-aligned posture and a return to an isolationist stage by the mid-1960s. This was the result of Chinese disillusionment with both superpowers. From Beijing's perspective, the United States had a conflictual posture in Southeast Asia, especially symbolized by the conflict in Vietnam.[56] Moscow also had shown a hegemonic tendency of its own and begun to put its national interests above the interests of the socialist camp. This became evident for many Chinese officials when Moscow opted for East–West détente which China perceived as irrelevant and harmful to the general struggle for national liberation.[57]

By utilizing the zone, the People's Republic of China aimed to undermine control of international affairs by the superpowers. This strategy was also evident in China's changing view of the United Nations, which it had earlier portrayed as the instrument of American and Soviet interests.[58] At the same time, China avoided involvement in any balance of power arrangement in either a global strategic alliance, like NAM, or a regional one, even in Indochina. Thus, one could assert that in a world of alignments, China acted more non-aligned than many official members of NAM. Moreover, China put more emphasis on the significance of the zone as its opposition to the superpowers grew.[59]

TRENDS IN CHINESE FOREIGN RELATIONS

Characterizing Chinese foreign policy as hostile for the entire first crucial decade following the 1949 Revolution is an oversimplification of a sophisticated and complex subject. Rather, the foreign relations of Revolutionary China exhibited three distinct trends.[60] It started with a two-track policy toward the superpowers from the triumph of the revolution (1 October 1949) to the start of the Korean War (25 June 1950). The next phase consisted of a conflictual posture, especially toward the United States, beginning on 25 October 1950 when China formally entered the war. Finally, a more conciliatory posture began on 29 April 1954 when China and India jointly declared the Five Principles of Peaceful Co-existence.[61] This declaration was a diplomatic signal to the West, particularly the United States, that China was ready for more cooperative relations.

A Two-Track Policy: 1949–1950

Soon after the revolution,[62] China pursued a two-track foreign policy toward the superpowers. The purpose of this policy was to distance itself from the United States,[63] while establishing closer ties with its so-called ideological "big brother," the Soviet Union. Moscow was seen as a friend,[64] despite its ill advice,[65] the uneasy relationship it had had with the Chinese Communist Party in prerevolutionary China,[66] and its ties with the Kuomintang.[67] It is important to mention that since the 1899 Spanish-American War, America's growing presence in Asia was watched carefully. Washington had some consideration for Beijing in its Asian policy. This became more evident as America's involvement in Asian affairs increased. In addition, national interest at the time required an anti-European colonial power and a pro-indigenous nationalistic stance in United States foreign policy in the region in order to open up a sphere of influence for the United States. Washington's strategic alignment with Beijing, however, did not have mass appeal. American leaders often had close associations with Chinese political elite—namely, Western-educated Chiang Kai-shek and his supporters. Meanwhile, the United States in the Far East maintained its animosity toward all socialist parties.[68]

In his speech of 30 June 1949, Mao Zedong described Beijing's growing ties with Moscow as "lean to one side,"[69] which sounded to Western ears like an alliance with the Soviets. The purpose of this policy, however, was not to make China a typical Soviet satellite state, but to create a working relationship between the People's Republic of China and the Soviet Union for protecting the new regime and furthering the revolutionary cause throughout the world.[70] This relationship engendered the optimism among the Chinese revolutionary leaders. As one expert stated:

> There was considerable optimism among the Chinese leaders that the Communist movement was soon to triumph in the other underprivileged countries and they may have hoped that the Soviet Union would keep the United States at bay while forces of socialist liberation in Asia and Africa, inspired by the Chinese example, launched their own struggles for freedom.[71]

The tone of Chinese foreign relations with the superpowers was set in part by the reaction of each to the establishment of the People's Republic of China on 1 October. Moscow immediately recognized the new regime, while Washington issued a statement reaffirming its recognition of the government of the Republic of China as the only official representative of all Chinese. Understandably, American reaction disappointed the Red Chinese.

The type of Chinese leaders was another factor in setting the tone of foreign relations. In general, more pragmatic revolutionary leaders, empowered by the success of the revolution, were increasingly controlling the political agenda.

Among this group, a well-known figure was Zhou Enlai who was unique in many respects. Zhou was a highly cultured, sophisticated, rational, realistic, and diplomatically talented individual. These qualities and characteristics led the Central People's Government (CPG) Council to appoint him as premier of the Government Administration Council (GAC) and the minister of foreign affairs of the CPG in its first meeting.[72]

The Chinese leaders, even the pragmatic Zhou, reacted accordingly to the different diplomatic gestures of the Great Powers.[73] On 3 October, Zhou Enlai welcomed the institutionalization of diplomatic relations with Moscow and the exchange of ambassadors. Within the next four weeks, Beijing seemed to be joining the Eastern camp as Zhou began to set up a network of friendly states, which included Bulgaria, Romania, Hungary, Czechoslovakia, North Korea, Poland, Mongolia, and East Germany.

Meanwhile, the United States was in a state of self-criticism over the loss of China, as the publication of the China White Papers indicated. For instance, the "Letter of Transmittal" to President Truman reveals a tendency to view the whole problem in American rather than Chinese terms, as shown by reference to "democratic individualism."[74] Beijing's indirect message to Washington, however, was evident in Zhou's cable of 15 November to the United Nations, which rejected the claim of Chiang Kai-shek's government to represent mainland China and declared that only the PRC government could do so. It is also important to point out that although the People's Republic of China maintained distanced relations with the United States, the Chinese realist leaders did not want to cut all ties with the West and advised Mao accordingly. One observer pronounced: "Mao was careful not to exclude the possibility of loans on terms of mutual benefit in the future from the capitalist power."[75]

Nevertheless, Mao's visit to the Soviet Union on 16 December 1949 and his meeting with Stalin seemed more newsworthy to most Western journalists than the encouraging diplomatic climate that existed between Beijing and some Western European capitals. This included London's and Oslo's notifying Beijing in early January of 1959 of their intentions to establish diplomatic relations. On 27 March, the Netherlands informed the People's Republic of China of its willingness to establish diplomatic ties. Also, Sweden, Denmark, and Switzerland formally established diplomatic relations with Revolutionary China, on 9 and 11 May and 14 September 1950.

Generally speaking, there was a divergence between American policy and that of the Europeans, who were interested in some kind of working relations with the CCP. The best example is the policy conflict between Washington and London regarding China.[76] From a Chinese perspective, it seems that there was a double standard by the Western media. When China showed interest in economic ties with the West, such news did not make it to the first page of any newspaper, but Mao's visiting Moscow was a newsworthy event. Meanwhile, the prolonged negotiations inspired by this visit led to the signing on 14 February 1950 of the Treaty of Friendship, Alliance, and Mutual Assistance.[77] Although Beijing's alignment with Moscow was partially based on China's ideological preferences, it was mainly for obvious strategic and economic reasons.[78] In other words, the Revolutionary Chinese were more pragmatic, rational, and logical in pursuing that policy than they were given credit by the West.

The gap between Washington and Beijing continued to widen in 1950 as their attitudes toward each other hardened or, in Mao's terms, their contradictions[79] intensified. On 14 January, in continuing the distancing process politically with Washington, Beijing took over the U.S. compound in the city, and the State Department ordered all its personnel in China to leave. The relationship deteriorated further in the early phase of the Cold War (especially after the signing of the Sino–Soviet friendship treaty), during the rise to power of Senator Joseph McCarthy, and most significantly when the Korean War began on 25 June 1950. Two days later, President Truman instructed the Seventh Fleet to prevent any possible attack on Taiwan. This was a change from President Truman's statement of 5 January on the status of Taiwan.[80]

The People's Republic of China responded by denouncing the American move as aggression and claimed that the island was an integral part of China. On 6 July, Zhou sent a message to the United Nations denouncing the resolution of the Security Council made on 27 June and calling on U.N. members to aid South Korea. On 27 August, Zhou cabled Secretary Dean Acheson protesting the intrusion into Chinese airspace by American planes and demanding compensation for the damages to Chinese territory from bombing near the border with Korea. These gestures by the United States played into the hands of Chinese hard-liners, who began to set the policy agenda. Due to America's ignoring earlier Chinese conciliatory gestures, the voice of the more pragmatic element began to whither. Soon, the hard-liners began to set the tone and the context of the policy agenda.

A Conflictual Trend: 1950 to Mid–1953

China's decision on 25 October to enter the Korean War ended the two-track policy period. It triggered a new era during which Beijing was more willing to use force to achieve its policy goals. In fact, some scholars have criticized American foreign policy for pressuring Revolutionary China to a point that it began to resort to confrontation by crossing the 38th parallel.[81] The Revolutionary Chinese were willing to show force not only in Korea, but also in other places. By the end of 1950, the People's Republic of China had already used troops to gain control of Tibet, but strong Tibetan resistance forced Beijing to utilize diplomacy on 23 May 1951 when it accepted the Agreement of the Liberation of Tibet. The Red Chinese had also resorted to military clashes against Macao in July of 1952, which ended on 23 August when China and Portugal settled the border dispute.

Whether the United States should take the blame for Chinese acts of aggression or the Chinese themselves, it is clear that there was a definite shift in Chinese foreign relations from benign to aggressive, despite international pressures. On 2 November, Chinese and American troops clashed in Korea for the first time. By the end of November, the Chinese forces, enjoying high morale, gained the military initiative and pushed the U.N. and South Korean forces south of the 38th parallel.

On 4 January 1951, Revolutionary China and North Korea captured Seoul, in spite of strong resistance by the U.N. forces, which were equipped with superior American hardware.

The U.S. Senate reacted to this development on 23 January by asking the United Nations to declare China an aggressor in Korea. Nine days later, the U.N. General Assembly adopted a U.S. sponsored resolution condemning Red China, which in turn denounced the U.N. measure.

The Beijing–Washington conflict had an economic dimension in addition to its political one. After Red China entered the Korean War, the United States froze all Chinese assets under its jurisdiction on 16 December 1950. It also prohibited trade with China.[82] Although the Chinese were desperate to have some economic relations with the West, they decided to reciprocate. This was accomplished twelve days later when the Government Administrative Council ordered the takeover of all U.S. property and froze U.S. assets in China.

In mid–March of 1951, the Chinese and North Korean troops evacuated Seoul in the face of strong pressure from the U.N. forces which were predominantly American. The United States also led the U.N. General Assembly to approve in May a worldwide embargo on the transportation of arms and war materials to Revolutionary China in May. Soon Dean Rusk, assistant secretary for Far Eastern affairs, reaffirmed that Washington did not recognize Beijing; instead it recognized Taipei.[83]

Throughout this period, the Chinese relied on Russian military supplies and especially on the Soviet diplomatic support at the United Nations to counteract American diplomatic initiatives.[84] The Russians, however, made a major diplomatic error in mid–January of 1950 when they boycotted the U.N. Security Council over the failure of their sponsored resolution to expel Taiwan from the United Nations. The Soviet boycott made it possible for the United States to build an international coalition within the U.N. system to use military measures against Red China and its North Korean ally.[85] If the boycott had not occurred, the international coalition would not have happened, and U.S. policy concerns about Revolutionary China could not have been legitimized by the international community. In addition, China would not have seen itself as a rogue state, struggling against the world order. Finally, the Korean War took its toll on Beijing. Soon, Chinese and North Korean forces showed signs of losing the military initiative, as their domestic structures became overwhelmed by the demands of the war. By 23 June 1951, the Chinese began to show more policy flexibility, which led the Russians to begin a new diplomatic initiative as the Russian U.N. delegate proposed cease-fire negotiations to end the war. It is worth mentioning that during the Korean War years, Sino–Soviet relations were the closest ever; yet, Beijing and Moscow had major problems in their relationship.[86]

Sino–American relations continued to be tense in the first quarter of 1953 the Chinese shot down an American airplane in northeastern China (12 January) and took the eleven survivors prisoner. On 2 February, President Dwight D. Eisenhower reversed the American policy at the time and announced that Taiwan could be used as a base of operations against Communist China. During the

Conference of the National Committee of Chinese People's Political Consultative Conference (CPPCC) five days later, Mao, with the support of radical idealists, responded by calling for a more intense struggle against the United States in Korea. He also adamantly encouraged the study of Marxism and Soviet history. In mid–February, the Chinese shot down five more American aircraft over northeastern China. Soon, the tension accelerated so rapidly that even the pragmatic Zhou accused the United States of sponsoring raids on China by Chiang Kai-shek's supporters and of turning Japan into a military base against the People's Republic.

From the Chinese perspective, the Korean War was a total war. As such, it was severely straining domestic resources, and pressuring the Chinese hard-liners.[87] Their grip over the policy process was loosening and Stalin's death in March of 1953 served as a catalyst for more pragmatic leaders to set the political agenda.[88] Thus, on 11 April the belligerents in the Korean War signed the Agreement for the Repatriation of Sick and Injured Captured Personnel. On 7 July, China, North Korea, and the U.N. Command signed an armistice at Panmunjom and issued a cease-fire order. Chinese troops began to return home.[89]

These events signaled a more conciliatory posture in Chinese foreign policy as realistic leaders began to set the political agenda. In addition to Zhou Enlai, the realistic faction included Liu Shaoqi and Deng Xiaoping. These leaders, who were also known as reformers, had consistently advocated more pragmatic options in policymaking during different periods of Chinese postrevolutionary history.[90] By 28 September, Beijing made some positive gestures toward the West. For example, the most prominent revolutionary realist at the time, Foreign Minister Zhou, stated that Beijing wanted diplomatic relations with Tokyo, but Japanese ties with Chiang Kai-shek's regime were blocking such efforts. He added that trade and cultural exchanges should be encouraged even without diplomatic relations. In October, responding to the demands of more pragmatic Chinese leaders, Mao approved an earlier Soviet proposal (28 September) for a conference of the foreign ministers of China, France, the United Kingdom, the United States, and the Soviet Union to discuss measures to ease international tension. Thus, the focus was clearly on utilizing more diplomatic negotiations and less military force.

Meanwhile, within the CCP, different factions were growing. By early February 1954, Liu Shaoqi was forced to call for party unity[91] of contending ideological tendencies between the revolutionary realists and idealists within the CCP intensified.[92] On domestic issues, the contest was between those who advocated a centralized power structure verses those leaders who supported a decentralized system. On foreign policy matters, there were those who wanted to make the world safe for the revolution (i.e., revolutionary idealists) who advocated the export of the revolution by any means, even armed struggle. On the other side were more pragmatic policymakers (i.e., revolutionary realists) who asked for improved diplomatic ties with all Great Powers so Revolutionary China could concentrate on building the new socialist state. They believed that the achievement of revolutionary goals at home would consequently export revolution by example. It should be noted that among the top five leaders—Mao Zedong, Liu Shaoqi, Zhou Enlai, Zhu De, and Ren Bishi, Liu and Zhou were more realistic leaders than the others. There was a shifting balance between the top idealistic and realistic leaders, especially after the premature death of Ren Bishi in 1950.

A Conciliatory Posture: 1954–1958

Long before the 1970s, China had shown accommodating diplomatic signals to the West, particularly the United States, in order to improve its ties. In this respect, 1954 was a significant year for the Chinese not because the government finally adopted the Constitutional draft in June. Of more significance was a shift in Beijing's strategy to soften its rugged diplomacy and increase its willingness to participate in substantive negotiations. On 20 April 1954, Zhou Enlai headed the Chinese delegation for the Conference on Korea and Indochina in Geneva,[93] where the People's Republic of China and six other states agreed to the Final Declaration of the Geneva Conference. The latter laid down a cease-fire agreement in Indochina and the division of Vietnam along the 17th parallel on 21 July. Also, in June Chinese and American representatives started to meet in Geneva for preliminary talks on problems relating to residents of the two states.[94]

The main symbol of the change in Chinese strategy, however, had come earlier on 29 April when China and India signed the agreement to invoke the Five Principles of Peaceful Coexistence. The treaty consisted of mutual respect for sovereignty and territorial integrity, mutual non-aggression, non-interference in each other's internal affairs, equality and mutual benefit, and peaceful coexistence. The significance of these principles was that they later became a part of the ideological foundation of the Non-Alignment Movement.[95] China affirmed its relations with other states based on these five principles in a joint communiqué with India. Later, other states joined China to affirm these principles, including Burma (29 June 1954), Cambodia (10 February 1956), and Laos (25 August 1956).

Beijing's more cooperative posture was especially evident toward those Third World states that were pursuing a non-alignment strategy in their foreign relations. The People's Republic of China perceived these states as potential allies in a united front style strategy that demonstrated an independent Chinese policy, one free from Soviet influence. This point was also identified by one Western expert during the Cold War, although it did not make an impression on most Western policymakers: "The consolidation of the American defensive system in Southeast Asia gave impetus to China's policy of seeking a modus vivendi with neutralist states. Its position enhanced by the Geneva settlement, the People's Republic took a leading part in a conference of Afro–Asian heads of state at Bandung in April 1955."[96] Thus, Beijing courted and established diplomatic ties with some of the more prominent Third World states. For example, China and Yugoslavia (on 10 January) and China and Afghanistan (on 20 January 1955) agreed to establish diplomatic relations. Opposed to earlier isolationist trends set by the hard-liners, China participated in the Asian Countries' Conference held in New Delhi in April of 1955. China also played an active and positive role in the Afro–Asian Conference held in Bandung. Contrary to China's earlier role in increasing tensions in Korea, Zhou expressed concern about the sense of international tension, instability, and vulnerability of Asian states. The constructive role of the Chinese delegation to this conference is clearly implied in the proceedings of the NAM documents.[97]

Zhou stated that the Five Principles were the cornerstone of China's foreign policy. In this respect, he clearly said:

> India, Burma, and China have affirmed the Five Principles of Peaceful Co-existence as the guiding principles in their mutual relations. These principles have received support from more and more countries. Following these principles, China and Indonesia have already achieved good results in their preliminary talks on the question of the nationality of citizens of one country residing in the other. During the Geneva Conference, China also expressed its readiness to develop friendly relations with Indo–Chinese states on the basis of these five principles. There is no reason why the relations between China and Thailand, the Philippines and other neighboring countries cannot be improved on the basis of these five principles ... China is [also] ready to establish normal relations with other Asian and African countries on the basis of the strict adherence to these principles and willing to promote the normalization of relations between China and Japan.[98]

In the closing session of the conference, Zhou stunned everyone by indicating China's willingness to negotiate with the United States, especially on the issue of Taiwan, in order to relax tensions between the two countries.[99] It is unfortunate that China's conciliatory posture was not recognized at the time by Western observers in general and Americans in particular because it could have led to significantly improved Sino–American relations well before the 1972 landmark visit by President Nixon. Although this positive signal led to the start of ambassadorial talks between Wang Bingnan and U. Alexis Johnson in August, it only touched the surface of problems regarding Sino–American relations. On 10 September, the two ambassadors announced an agreement on the return of civilians to their respective countries. A month later, a spokesman for the Chinese People's Volunteers Headquarters declared that nineteen divisions of its troops had withdrawn completely from Korea by 26 October.[100]

Thus, despite these positive developments, the scope of the talks was rather limited and they failed to address the overall ties between the two states. One can argue that the American policy shortcoming was to focus on the effects rather than causes of its problematic ties with China. Therefore, Sino–American relations were not normalized during this period despite China's positive attitude, mainly because of Secretary of State John Foster Dulles's inflexible Cold War world view.[101]

The conciliatory diplomatic signals by China indicated that its policy posture was moving from an offensive position to a defensive position. For instance, contrary to its earlier negative image of the world order in general and the United Nations in particular, the People's Republic of China also showed that it was willing to work within the international system and with international institutions. Long gone were the days when Mao, with the support of the idealists, continuously attacked the United Nations and the global status quo for which it stood. In this respect, a positive development was China's warm reception of Dag Hammarskjöld, secretary-general of the United Nations, in Beijing for talks with Zhou Enlai

(January of 1955) regarding efforts to decrease regional tension. Chinese leaders went out of their way by catering to this activist and controversial Secretary-General.[102] Another positive gesture by China was its active participation in the World Peace Assembly held in Helsinki in June of 1955.[103]

One major result of this active diplomacy was an increasingly confident attitude among the revolutionary leaders about their policy, as Mao's speech "On The Ten Major Relationships" illustrated on 25 April 1956. According to one specialist on China, this growing sense of confidence "allowed China to embark on the offshore islands probe with an assurance which horrified its Soviet ally."[104] In fact, this overconfident attitude may have led to the swing to the idealistic tendencies in China's foreign policy later, as the 1958 Island Crisis indicated. At the same time, the Chinese attitude became more positive about its international environment, especially during 1955 and 1956.[105]

By emphasizing more negotiations and less confrontation, Zhou expressed China's willingness to meet on 28 June with Taiwanese authorities to discuss the peaceful liberation of Taiwan. This gesture certainly indicated a departure from the past pattern of using the People's Liberation Army (PLA) as the main policy instrument of liberation of territories held by Chiang Kai-shek's or others' forces. It implied that the revolutionary realists had the upper hand in the formulation and implementation of foreign policy. This conclusion was confirmed by the outcome of the Eighth National Congress of the CCP, which adopted a revised Party Constitution. Although this document stated that the CCP followed Marxism-Leninism as its guide to action, it made no reference, however, to Mao's "Thoughts" which motivated many Chinese revolutionary idealists. This development also decreased the underlying tension in Sino–Soviet relations, which had intensified during the second stage of Chinese foreign policy.[106]

The year 1957 was a special one for Beijing-Moscow ties for Soviet accomplishments in missile technology and the launch of *Sputnik I* stunned America.[107] Chinese leaders were so impressed by Soviet technological developments that Mao confidently gave his "East Wind Over West Wind" speech during the fortieth anniversary of the October Revolution in Moscow.[108] The Chinese hoped that the Russians would share their technology, as was implied by the Sino–Soviet Agreement on New Technology for National Defense.[109] Time, however, proved that Moscow was not willing to share.

The Chinese revolutionary leaders tried to play the balancing act in their foreign policy between the socialist and non-socialist worlds. On 30 September, they hosted President Sukarno of Indonesia, the first non-communist head of state to visit Beijing. Although this gesture did not receive the attention it deserved from Western corners, it was very significant from the Chinese policy perspective. On 14 October, the two states issued a joint press communiqué on their common political and economic concerns. For the Chinese, Sukarno's visit signified improving relations with the non-socialist world, so they balanced this gesture by supporting the socialist camp. Soon, China issued a statement advocating a Soviet declaration on cooperation between Russia and other socialist countries.[110]

From the perspective of some in the West, however, China had taken a one-sided approach to its foreign policy by on the same day supporting the Soviet invasion of Hungary and denouncing the British and French aggression against Egypt. One should recall, however, that Washington also denounced the British and French invasion of the Suez, which is the same point that Beijing emphasized. Moreover, the United States did not help the Hungarian freedom fighters, despite words of encouragement to stand against Soviet hegemony, which were broadcasted throughout Eastern Europe over Voice of America. From this perspective, China's behavior does not seem so one-sided at the time.

We must also consider that Beijing saw the anti-socialist context of the pro-democracy Hungarians as a threat to the very survival of its own revolution and regime. In fact, one expert asserted that for Red China, the 1956 Hungarian Crisis was a disturbing consequence of the de-Stalinization process that General Secretary Nikita Khrushchev had started earlier.[111] Thus, China supported the military invasion of Hungary by the Warsaw Pact nations. Moreover, China's diplomatic support for Egypt was not surprising considering that this was part of its anti-colonial stance. These positions indicated China's independent foreign policy based upon a united front strategy with intermediate zones. Furthermore, the British–French invasion of Egypt followed Gamal Nasser's nationalization of the Suez Canal. Finally, for Third World states, these issues concerned the notion of complete independence that Beijing had already advocated on a number of occasions. For example, during his address at the Bandung Conference, Zhou Enlai sympathized with the Egyptians in their struggle to regain sovereignty over the Suez Canal.[112]

In 1957, the mainland Chinese also witnessed relaxation in the domestic political environment with the One Hundred Flowers Campaign, which reached its climax in May.[113] A regional development, however, changed the tide and made the revolutionary regime feel less secure and, consequently, less tolerant of domestic critics of the government. When the United States installed guided-missile units in Taiwan, the Chinese Ministry of Foreign Affairs strongly protested this American initiative. Soon the Anti-Rightist Campaign initiated by the hard-liners ended the period of freely criticizing CCP authorities.

In the Fourth Session of the First National People's Congress (NPC), Zhang Bojun, minister of communications, was directly and strongly criticized. In the same conference, Lu Dingyi and other hard-liners criticized the pragmatists, whom they labeled rightists. The hard-liners based their criticism on the April Rectification Campaign that the Chinese Communist Party had launched according to Mao's speech on contradiction and counter-revolutionaries in February.[114]

A Temporary Relapse to a Conflictual Posture

From the Chinese perspective, the introduction of this significant American military equipment was a direct threat to Chinese security. It was a provocative gesture that flew in the face of Chinese good-will efforts at the time.[115] This state of affairs was a setback for more pragmatic elements within the Chinese leadership. Consequently, soon the more idealistic leaders took the initiative, and the conflictual tendency in Chinese affairs made a comeback in 1958. One student of Chinese affairs called this the "Frantic Year."[116] In addition to the American initiative in Taiwan, another cause of this new conflictual tendency was the growing confidence among the Chinese revolutionary idealists as a result of Soviet scientific accomplishments. Thus, 1958 became a year of new experiments. In domestic affairs, the idealists, led by Mao, launched the Great Leap Forward. Their slogans advocated self-sufficiency in order to decrease Chinese dependence on the Soviets, to increase Red China's policy options, and to narrow China's modernization gap with the Great Powers. Finally, the domestic scene also witnessed changes in political personnel. Mao appointed Chen Yi as foreign minister to succeed Zhou Enlai in February. There were also other significant changes among the top government personnel in the first half of 1958. For example, on 31 January 1958, the NPC Standing Committee dismissed Minister of Communications, Zhang Bojun, and two other ministers as rightists. Chairman Mao confirmed these decisions.[117]

In foreign affairs, the conflictual posture was renewed in August as the islands crisis began when the PLA fired on the Taiwan-held island of Quemoy and disrupted shipping around Matsu Island.[118] On 4 September, the People's Republic of China declared that the breadth of the territorial sea of China was twelve nautical miles. This was a threat to American ships bringing supplies to Quemoy Island.[119] Secretary Dulles issued a statement on the American intention to support the defense of both islands against any attack by China. The tension was building in the region, and Beijing did not receive support from Moscow during this crisis. The Soviets had already given China the signal that they would not approve a hostile liberation of Taiwan by the Chinese because such action would most likely increase the chance of a direct confrontation with the United States. This stance was apparent when the Sino–Soviet joint communiqué on 3 August at the conclusion of Khrushchev's visit made no mention of the Taiwan issue, though Beijing desperately needed Soviet support to neutralize American policy.

Soon, Zhou came up with a face-saving formula for both sides by simultaneously suggesting the resumption of Sino–American ambassadorial talks and reaffirming China's right to liberate its own territory. This point was sought by the hard-line leaders within the CCP. In response, on 30 September, Secretary Dulles suggested that if there were a dependable cease-fire in the area, it would be foolish to maintain a large number of Taiwanese forces on the islands. A week later, the Chinese minister of national defense announced a cease-fire, which effectively ended the crisis.

For the Chinese, the lessons learned from the offshore islands episode were important: the United States was strongly committed to supporting the Taiwanese regime, and the People's Republic of China could not count on Soviet assistance to liberate Taiwan.[120] The lack of Soviet dependability led to a more independent China. By the tenth anniversary of the 1949 Revolution, two major events taught Beijing to count even less on Moscow. The Tibet rebellion[121] and the U.S.–U.S.S.R. Détente both contributed to creating a more radical posture in Chinese foreign policy toward the superpowers.[122] Faced with perceived simultaneous internal and external threats, Revolutionary China began to exhibit less flexibility in its foreign relations, particularly toward the superpowers.

Even in a bipolar international system, the problems in Sino–Soviet relations did not quickly and necessarily translate into better Sino–American relations. A more conciliatory Chinese foreign policy posture was a necessary but in itself not sufficient condition for improving relations between the two countries. Due to American foreign policy goals during this period, the United States was not willing or could not afford to show conciliatory gestures toward China in order to establish normal diplomatic ties. After the armistice in Korea, the United States became increasingly fearful of communist advances in Indochina. Secretary Dulles's address to the Overseas Press Club on the eve of the Geneva Conference in March of 1954 represented the American attitude toward the People's Republic of China.[123]

The Americans had not forgotten the Munich lesson, learned in the late–1930s, and Washington was not willing to offer Revolutionary China an accommodating strategy that could have been misinterpreted as another Munich appeasement policy. In fact, Washington's containment strategy was to prevent the expansion of communism and accordingly it created a chain of regional security organizations around Red China. In addition, the United States signed a number of bilateral security and defense treaties with some key Southeast Asian states. One example was the establishment in September of 1954 of the Southeast Asia Treaty Organization (SEATO) by the United States, the United Kingdom, France, Australia, New Zealand, the Philippines, Thailand, and Pakistan. SEATO's goal was to contain communist aggression of either an overt or subversive nature.[124]

As a result, Sino–American relations did not significantly improve until 1972, three years after Sino–Soviet border clashes took place and two years after the establishment of relations between China and Canada.[125] This late response to improving ties with China was primarily due to American involvement in Vietnam and a lack of foreign policy foresight. The latter has led some experts to suggest that the changing relations between China and the United States since 1972, combined with the shock expressed by Americans over the Tiananmen tragedy, require an American bipartisan consensus as far as Sino–American policy is concerned.[126] Secretary Henry Kissinger deserves much of the credit for renewing relations with China during his imaginative secret trip to Beijing in 1971.[127]

CONCLUSION

This study indicates that Chinese foreign relations did not have a random nature as many assume. In fact, there were three distinct foreign policy behaviors: two-track, conflictual, and conciliatory. Thus, the foreign relations of the People's Republic of China should not be characterized simply as hostile for the entire first crucial decade following the 1949 Revolution. Considering the historical and cultural context of China from a "Chinacentric" perspective, it is understandable why Beijing has formulated and implemented its foreign policy. China's prerevolutionary modern history witnessed a proud nation and a great ancient civilization being humiliated by colonial Europeans, whom the Chinese considered to be barbarians. This experience was quite a rude political and cultural awakening for the Chinese, who have traditionally considered themselves the center of the universe or the middle kingdom.[128] From this perspective, leaders of the 1949 Revolution can be best described as nationalist at heart, although many of them used Marxist revolutionary rhetoric. The best evidence of this true nature is found in Mao's theory of semicolonialism.

This experience made the Chinese revolutionary leaders, especially Mao, sensitive to American and European involvement in their affairs.[129] For instance, during the first stage of the postrevolutionary era, Red China tried to distance itself from the United States because it perceived the overwhelming American military presence in the Far East to be too close for comfort to the infant revolutionary regime. In the conflictual period, Chinese leaders were greatly concerned about the presence of U.N. troops, predominately American, near their traditional sphere of influence in Korea. Confident and optimistic about the state's power and public morale, the idealistic Chinese leaders decided to respond to these threats by projecting their power and utilizing their military might instead of pursuing diplomatic negotiations. Then, starting in 1953 Chinese realist leaders began to set the policy tone. They believed that external pressures, in combination with domestic challenges, were overwhelming and began to emphasize a more cooperative posture rather than a conflictual one. This change in stance was evident in both the actions and words of the leadership.

My discussion of the Chinese foreign policy perspective also shows that the Chinese were using a balancing act strategy in order to keep their policy options open. In this respect, Beijing first employed this strategy to keep the United States at bay by borrowing the Soviet's security umbrella during the revolutionary regime's infancy. However, toward the end of the decade, when the revolutionary regime was well-institutionalized and solidified, they actively pursued friendships with the Western powers and opened up more channels to prominent Third World states in order to reduce strategic and diplomatic dependency on Moscow.

It is essential to emphasize that despite their revolutionary rhetoric, the Chinese leaders had given a number of positive diplomatic signals to the West, especially the United States, in the first decade after the Revolution. Some of these signals were identified by Washington and some were not recognized. Even those signals that were clearly communicated did not necessarily lead to a complete overhaul of Sino–American relations. This lack of action cannot be blamed solely on China. America must also accept its responsibility since the United States was not willing or could not afford to appease Revolutionary China, fearing that such actions could send a wrong message during a period of intense Cold War.

Lessons learned from the analysis of the early period following the 1949 Revolution are in some ways applicable to present-day China, which on the surface seems quite different from Mao's China. My discussion indicates that four factors are worth emphasizing and can be used to understand and estimate Chinese foreign policy behavior. The first factor is the type of leader—revolutionary realist or idealist. Realistic leaders tend to be willing to work within the current international structure and institutions. They realize their state's power limits and are more willing to compromise to reach their policy goals. On the other hand, idealistic leaders are those who see the success of the revolution as a stepping stone in a series of upheavals against enemies, both inside and outside the country. With their outward-looking perspective, many idealists challenge their international environments. Their anti-status quo rhetoric often poses a threat to the national security of other states, especially in the first few years after the revolution.

The second factor is how the issue at hand is defined—as a domestic one or foreign policy concern. If the problem is defined as domestic in nature, Chinese leaders are less willing to negotiate on the issue and more willing to use force. If it is defined, however, as having a foreign dimension, the leaders show a tendency to compromise. A recent example of this is China's release of human rights activist Harry Wu after he was convicted in their courts. The evidence also indicates that in terms of Chinese economic relations, from the start of the revolution Beijing has always been more willing to deal with the West. Moreover, the Chinese are more willing to accommodate foreign demands over some of the most controversial economic issues. In the case of copyright laws, Chinese leaders have shown a willingness to negotiate.

The third variable that I identify is the intensity of pressure on the domestic structure of the country at the time. Evidence illustrates that the leadership tends to be more conciliatory in conducting foreign policy when it faces a major domestic challenge or mounting domestic pressures. For instance, when Chinese economic and military sectors became overwhelmed by the military pressures put on them by the United Nations in Korea, Mao yielded to the more pragmatic leaders by opting to negotiate. Similarly, the failure of the Great Leap Forward contributed to conciliatory gestures made by China at the end of the decade.

The fourth factor is the degree of foreign support received by Beijing. When China enjoyed the friendship of the Soviets, it was less willing to compromise with the United States. This position can also be attributed to Beijing's balancing act strategy, using one superpower against the other as far as that power is willing to play the game. Take the Korean War, for example. While China had full military and diplomatic support of the Soviet Union, it had less reason to negotiate. During the island crisis, however, Chinese leaders soon realized that they could not rely on Soviet support. Thus, the more pragmatic Zhou stole the center stage from idealistic leaders by redefining the situation and coming up with a compromise for both sides. This shift in power was evident by the unexpected willingness of the Chinese to negotiate instead of continuing to disrupt shipping near the island.

It is also important to note that the more international pressure Beijing receives on domestic issues, the more introverted and the less willing to compromise it becomes. For example, the international community has pressured China to improve its human rights practices; yet, little progress has been made. Beijing is willing to compromise only on those cases that have a significant foreign dimension.

NOTES

1. Throughout this chapter, I use the designations China, Red China, Revolutionary China, and the People's Republic of China interchangeably. I use the term *Taiwan* to refer to the Republic of China on the Island of Formosa.

2. For example, see J. Richard Walsh, *Change, Continuity and Commitment: China's Adaptive Foreign Policy*, (Lanham, Md.: University Press of America, 1988), especially p. 1.

3. For a thoughtful account of Western selective perception of Chinese behavior, see Colin Mackerras, *Western Images of China* (Oxford: Oxford University Press, 1989).

4. For a careful cultural and political analysis of the Chinese modernization process, see Suzanne Ogden, *China's Unresolved Issues: Politics, Development, and Culture*, 3d ed. (Englewood Cliffs, N.J.: Prentice-Hall, 1995), especially pp. 311-48.

5. For a fresh and rare analysis of the Sino–American political clash from a contrasting cultural perspective, see Richard Madsen, *China and the American Dream: A Moral Inquiry* (Berkeley: University of California Press, 1995).

6. America's perception of Chinese affairs was also tainted prior to the establishment of Revolutionary China. For more information about the Cold War era and on prerevolutionary China, see Odd Arne Westad, *Cold War and Revolution: Soviet-American Rivalry and the Origins of the Chinese Civil War, 1944–1946* (New York: Columbia University Press, 1993).

7. See the publication of Mao's doctor, Li Zhisui, *The Private Life of Chairman Mao: The Memoirs of Mao's Personal Physician Dr. Li Zhisui* translated by Tai Hung-chao (New York: Random House, 1989).

8. Mao Zedong, "On Contradiction," *Selected Works of Mao Tse-Tung*, vol. 1 (Peking: Foreign Languages Press, 1969), 313.

9. John Gittings, *The World and China, 1922–1972*, (New York: Harper and Row, 1974), 37.

10. Ibid., 43.

11. Ibid., 38.

12. Ibid., 39.

13. Mao integrated the concept of united front" into Marxism in his major work on dialectics, "On Contradiction" (see Mao, *Selected Works*, vol. 1).

14. For a full text of Mao's 30 June 1949 speech, see *Selected Works of Mao Tse-tung*, vol. 4, 415-17.

15. For a detailed record of the concept of united front in China, see Lyman P. Van Slyke, *Enemies and Friends: The United Front in Chinese Communist History* (Stanford, Calif.: Stanford University Press, 1967).

16. It must be mentioned that China's definition of hegemony has changed over time. While it originally referred to military intervention, since 1982 it also began to include political interference. See Lillian C. Harris and Robert L. Worden, eds. *China and the Third World: Champion or Challenger?* (Dover, Mass.: Auburn House, 1986), 128.

17. For example, one can find references to the enemy in *Romance of the Three Kingdoms*, vol. 2, translated by C. H. Brewitt-Taylor (Oxford: Oxford University Press, 1925), 612-14.

18. Lenin, one of the founders of the Communist Party of Soviet Union (CPSU), is most likely the modern originator of the united front strategy, although the term was not actually used in communist writings until the 1920s. V. I. Lenin, "What Is To Be Done," *Collected*

Works, vol. 5 (London: Lawrence & Wishart, 1961), especially 362-75.

19. As early as 1922, the CCP indicated that it was possible to form a united front with the nationalists, particularly the Kuomintang (KMT), to fight the colonial powers. See Ch'en Kung-po, *The Communist Movement in China* (New York: Columbia University Press, 1960), 120).

20. For example, Voitinsky (chief Comintern agent in China) had urged the party to recognize three groups within the Nationalist Party—Left, Right, and Center. The CCP was advised to align with the Left, gain some support from the Center, and oppose the Right. See C. Martin Wilbur and Julie Lien-ying Howe, *Documents on Communism, Nationalism, and Soviet Advisers in China 1918–1927* (New York: Columbia University Press, 1956), 89. The same strategy was accepted for the conducting of foreign policy.

21. J. D. Armstrong, *Revolutionary Diplomacy: Chinese Foreign Policy and the United Front Doctrine* (Berkeley: University of California Press, 1977), 13.

22. Mao, "On Policy," *Selected Works*, vol. 2, 289.

23. Mao, "On Contradiction," *Selected Works*, vol. 1, 331.

24. Armstrong, 36.

25. Allen S. Whiting, *China Crosses the Yalu* (Stanford, Calif.: Stanford University Press, 1960).

26. For such views about Chinese intentions, see John Gittings, "The Great Power Triangle and Chinese Foreign Policy," *China Quarterly*, (July-September 1969).

27. For a discussion of the definition of the concept of alliance, see Ole R. Holsti, P. Terrence Hopmann, and John D. Sullivan, *Unity and Disintegration in International Alliance* (New York: Wiley, 1973), 3-4.

28. See Mao's 30 June 1949 speech in *Selected Works*, vol. 4, pp. 15-17.

29. Ibid.

30. For instance, see Mao's 30 June 1949 speech.

31. Ibid.

32. Joseph Camilleri, *Chinese Foreign Policy: The Maoist Era and its Aftermath* (Oxford: Martin Robertson, 1980), 47.

33. Samuel Kim, ed., *China and the World*, 2d ed. (Boulder. Colo.: Westview Press, 1989), 60.

34. Gittings, *World and China*, 151.

35. Ibid., 150-51.

36. Soon Ching-Ling (Madame Sun Yat-Sen) "The Difference Between Soviet and American Foreign Policies," *People's China* 1, no. 2 (16 January 1950): 5-8.

37. Camilleri, 49.

38. See "Long Live Mao Tse-tung's Thought," translated by the Joint Publications Research Service under the title "Miscellany of Mao Tse-tung Thought (1949–1968)" parts 1 and 2, JPRS no. 61269 (1974), 256.

39. Gittings, *World and China*, 153.

40. Ibid., 154.

41. For a full text of the treaty, see *Sino-Soviet Treaty and Agreements* (Peking: Foreign Languages Press, 1950), 5-8.

42. Kim, 60.

43. Gittings, *World and China*, 155.

44. Kim, 59.

45. Camilleri, 48.

46. On the nature, scope, and major assumptions of convergence of interest, see chapter 4.

47. Gittings, *World and China*, 219.

48. Ibid., 9.

49. For example, see the view of Maoist Yu Chao-li, a *Red Flag* commentator on 16 August 1958 in Gittings, *World and China*, 219.

50. See Mao's 30 June 1949 speech.

51. Gittings, *World and China*, 234.

52. For an analysis of this perspective of the Chinese world view, see John K. Fairbank, "A Preliminary Framework," in *The Chinese World Order: Traditional China's Foreign Relations*, ed. John F. Fairbank (Cambridge: Harvard University Press, 1968).

53. Camilleri, 17.

54. An editorial article from *People's Daily*, 21 January 1964, in , 24 January 1964, p. 7.

55. *Red Flag* no. 11 November 1972 in *Peking Review*, vol. 15, no. 45 (10 November 1972), cited in Lawrance, 231.

56. Gittings, *World and China*, 220.

57. Ibid., 9.

58. Camilleri, 20.

59. Gittings, *World and China*. 233.

60. Throughout this section, I have relied on the following source for the exact dates of major events in Chinese affairs: Colin Mackerras, *Modern China: A Chronology from 1842 to the Present* (London: Thames and Hudson, 1982).

61. For a recent comprehensive study of Beijing–New Delhi relations, see Xuecheng Liu, *The Sino–Indian Border Dispute and Sino–Indian Relations* (Lanham, Md.: University Press of America, 1994).

62. For a classical analysis of the causes of the Chinese Revolution see Lucien Bianco, *Origins of the Chinese Revolution 1915–1949* (Stanford, Calif.: Stanford University Press, 1967). Also, for a work looking at the causes of the revolution from different perspectives and using a number of variables, see Kathleen Hartford and Steven M. Goldstein, eds., *Single Sparks* (Armonk, N.Y.: M. E. Sharpe, 1989).

63. In this respect, close relations with the United States is reminiscent of the traditional dominance of the Western European powers in China. For a summary of China's prerevolutionary experience with the European powers, see Gittings, *World and China*, 17-65. For a detailed account of Sino–American prerevolutionary relations, see Charles R. Kitts, *The United States Odyssey in China, 1784 –1990* (Lanham, Md.: University Press of America, 1991).

64. Or at least the lesser of the two "evils," if one adopts Tai Hung-chao's book.

65. For example, the CPSU advised the CCP to focus on the cities during the 1930s and 1940s. The CCP, however, could not match the firepower of the KMT and suffered significantly after the KMT began to suppress it. See Suzanne Ogden, *China*, Global Studies Series, 4th ed., vol. 12 (Guilford, Conn.: Dushkin Publishing Group, 1991), 7.

66. For a discussion of the uneasy relationship between the Russian and Chinese communist movements, see Robert C. North, *Moscow and the Chinese Communists*, (Stanford, Calif.: Stanford University Press, 1953). Also, see John W. Garver, *Chinese–Soviet Relations, 1937–1945* (New York: Oxford University Press, 1988).

67. Some experts suggested that the Soviets were looking after their own interests from the early days of Revolutionary China. For example, see Lawrance, 21-22. On the Soviet ties to Nationalist Chinese, see C. Martin Wilbur and Julie Lien-ying Howe, *Missionaries of Revolution: Soviet Advisers and Nationalist China, 1920–1927* (Cambridge: Harvard

University Press, 1989). Also see Gordon H. Chang, *Friends and Enemies: The United States, China, and the Soviet Union, 1948–1972* (Stanford, Calif.: Stanford University Press, 1990).

68. For a critical view of Sino-American relations from 1899 to 1949, see Arnold Xiangze Jiang, *The United States and China* (Chicago: University of Chicago Press, 1988).

69. Mao's view of "lean to one side" was presented in his 30 June 1949 speech in *Selected Works of Mao*, vol. 4. For a discussion of Mao's foreign policy decision making based on "lean to one side," see Camilleri, 47.

70. An extensive account of Sino–Soviet relations from 1945–1990 can be found in Lowell Dittmer, *Sino–Soviet Normalization and Its International Implications, 1945–1990*, (Seattle: University of Washington Press, 1992).

71. Lawrance, 15.

72. For an introductory text on the significant role of Zhou in the early years of revolution, see Lucian W. Pye, *China: An Introduction* 4th ed. (New York: Harper Collins, 1991), 223-27.

73. For a comprehensive analysis of Zhou Enlai's leadership in conducting Chinese foreign policy, see Ronald C. Keith, *The Diplomacy of Zhou Enlai* (New York: St. Martin's Press, 1989).

74. See *United States Relations With China* (Washington, D.C.: Department of State, 1949), xvi-xvii.

75. Lawrence, 15.

76. In this regard see Chang, chapter 2, especially pp. 42-44.

77. For its text, see *Sino–Soviet Treaty and Agreements* (Peking: Foreign Languages Press, 1950), 5-8.

78. Camilleri, 48-49.

79. For Mao's view on contradictions, refer to Mao Tse-tung, "On Contradiction," The Selected Works, 313.

80. *American Foreign Policy 1950–1955*, vol. 1 (Washington, D.C.: Department of State, 1957), 2448-49.

81. For example, see K. M. Panikkar, *In Two Chinas, Memoirs of a Diplomat* (London: Allen and Unwin, 1955), 109-11.

82. Lawrence, 47.

83. Franz Schurmann and Orville Schell, *Communist China: Revolutionary Reconstruction and International Confrontation (1949 to the Present)* (New York: Vintage Books, 1966), 298.

84. For more information, see Jian Chen, *The Sino–Soviet Alliance and China's Entry into the Korean War*, (Washington, D.C.: Cold War International History Project, Woodrow Wilson International Center for Scholars, 1992).

85. Another implication of the boycott, according to one expert, was the endangerment of the whole U.N. system. For more information about this, see Inis L. Claude, Jr., *Swords into Plowshares*, 4th ed. (New York: Random House, 1984), 157-58.

86. For more information, see Sergei N. Goncharov, John W. Lewis, and Xue Litai, *Uncertain Partners: Stalin, Mao, and the Korean War* (Stanford, Calif.: Stanford University Press, 1993).

87. Regarding the domestic stress of the regime, see Robert Garson, *The United States and China Since 1949, A Troubled Affair* (Madison Teanek, United Kingdom: Fairleigh Dickinson University Press, 1994), 41-42. This source also indicates that the Beijing government had a hostile posture in dealing with domestic affairs, in addition to its

conflictual behavior in foreign policy, especially in Korea, pp. 40-43.

88. On the impact of Stalin's leadership in Chinese affairs, see Brian Murray, *Stalin, the Cold War, and the Division of China: A Multi-Archival Mystery* (Washington, D.C.: Cold War International History Project, Woodrow Wilson International Center for Scholars, 1995).

89. For an analysis of the Korean conflict, see Gittings, *World and China*, 180-95. Also see Harvey W. Nelsen, *Power and Insecurity: Beijing, Moscow, and Washington, 1949–1988* (Boulder, Colo.: Lynne Rienner, 1989), 8-12.

90. For instance, see Garson, 86-87.

91. On the role and nature of Liu Shaoqi within the CCP structure, see Pye, 227-29. For a detailed analysis of his leadership, see Lowell Dittmer, *Liu Shao-chi and the Chinese Cultural Revolution* (Berkeley: University of California Press, 1974).

92. For more information on the significance of Liu Shaoqi and the role he played later in the Cultural Revolution, see Bill Brugger, *China: Radicalism to Revisionism, 1962–1979* (London: Croom Helm, 1981), especially chapter 2.

93. A sign of the new trend was evident by the constructive role of Zhou in the conference. See Harold C. Hinton, *Communist China in World Politics* (London: Macmillan, 1966), 252-54.

94. On Sino-American diplomatic talks, see K. J. Young, *Negotiating With the Chinese Communist: The United States Experience, 1953–1967*, (New York: McGraw-Hill, 1968), 7-9.

95. On 23 April 1955, Zhou presented these principles to the Political Committee of the Bandung Conference (*New York Times*, 25 April 1955, p. 7).

96. Lawrance, 18.

97. In this regard, see *Asia-Africa Speaks From Bandung* (Djakarta, Indonesia: The Ministry of Foreign Affairs, Republic of Indonesia, 1955), 58-59.

98. Ibid., 62.

99. Ibid., 181.

100. Mackerras, *Modern China*, 468.

101. Lawrance, 64.

102. For more information about Hammarskjöld's controversial life which led to his so-called accidental death during the Congo Crisis, see Robert S. Jordan, ed., *Dag Hammarskjöld Revisited* (Durham: Carolina Academic Press, 1983).

103. Shen Yanbing, the minister of culture, led the Chinese delegation and Guo Moruo attended as vice-president of the World Peace Council (see Mackerras, *Modern China*, 466).

104. Gittings, 202.

105. Ibid.

106. For a brief analysis of the Sino–Soviet rift, see John Gittings, *World and China*, 141-62. For a comprehensive analysis of Sino–Soviet ties, see Lowell Dittmer, *Sino–Soviet Normalization*.

107. John T. Rourke, *Making Foreign Policy: United States, Soviet Union, and China* (Pacific Grove, Calif.: Brooks/Cole Publishing, 1990), 19.

108. For the full text, see *Peking Review* (6 September 1963): 10.

109. The agreement, based on the Chinese statement of 15 August 1963, promised China a sample of the Soviet A-bomb (Mackerras, *Modern China*, 480).

110. October 30 was the day Soviet reinforcements entered Hungary against the government of Imre Nagy. The text of this statement was transcribed in *Department of State Bulletin* 35, no. 907 (12 November 1956): 745-46.

111. See Lawrance, 65.

112. See *Asia-Africa Speaks From Bandung*, 60.

113. Roderick MacFarguhar, *The Hundred Flowers Campaign and the Chinese Intellectuals* (New York: Octagon, 1973), first printed in 1960.

114. On the anti-rightist struggle and lessons of the Rectification Campaign, see Schurmann and Schell, 155-60.

115. Garson, 74-75.

116. Pye, 248-52.

117. See Mackerras, *Modern China*, 485.

118. On Chinese military policy, see John Gittings, *The Role of the Chinese Army* (London: Oxford University Press, 1967); and Samuel B. Griffith II, *The Chinese People's Liberation Army* (New York: McGraw-Hill, 1967).

119. For a comprehensive and comparative analysis of the offshore Island Crisis, see Charles A. McClelland, et al., "The Communist Chinese Performance in Crisis and Non-Crisis: Quantitative Studies of the Taiwan Straits Confrontation 1950–1964," Report N60530-11207 to the Naval Ordnance Test Station (China Lake: U.S. Naval Ordnance Test Station, December 1965). According to the report, this type of crisis behavior differs somewhat from behavior in crises that escalate into full-scale war.

120. For an extensive analysis of relations within the "Strategic Triangle," see John G. Stroessinger, *Nations in Darkness: China, Russia, and America*, 5th ed. (New York: McGraw-Hill, 1990).

121. For a clear discussion of the Tibet Crisis, see George Patterson, "China and Tibet: Background to Revolt," *China Quarterly*, no. 1 (January-March 1960): 87-102.

122. A careful analysis of the events in the 1960s and 1970s is beyond the scope of this study. It is sufficient to say that China returned to a conflictual posture regarding both domestic and international affairs, as most Chinese historians have testified. The Cultural Revolution, which led to a great many radical policies and violent measures, dominated Chinese domestic affairs. And in foreign policy, the Sino–Soviet rift became visible, the Sino–Indian Border War occurred, and Revolutionary China began to actively export revolutionary policy in the Third World, particularly in Africa.

123. For the text of this speech, see *Department of State Bulletin* 30, (12 April 1954): 539-40.

124. On SEATO, see George Modelski, *SEATO: Six Studies* (Melbourne, Australia: F. W. Cheshire, 1962).

125. On territorial disputes and clashes, see George Ginsburgs and Carl F. Pinkele, *The Sino–Soviet Territorial Dispute, 1949–1964* (New York: Praeger, 1978).

126. For instance, see Gerrit Gong, *U.S. China Policy: Building a New Consensus* (Washington: The Center for Strategic and International Studies, 1994), especially pp. v-ix.

127. For Kissinger's view of China, see Henry Kissinger, *Years of Upheaval* (Boston: Little, Brown, 1982).

128. On the Chinese cultural and political context of relating to foreigners or barbarians, see Warren I. Cohen, *America's Response to China: A History of Sino–American Relations*, 3d ed. (New York: Columbia University Press, 1990), especially pp. 1-25.

129. For an analysis of Mao's leadership from a Chinese cultural and political perspective, see John E. Wills, Jr., *Mountain of Fame: Portraits in Chinese History* (Princeton: Princeton University Press, 1994), 335-59.

4

CUBAN FOREIGN RELATIONS, 1959–1969

Revolutionary Cuba in the 1959 to 1964 period is a fascinating case study for foreign policy analysts because it brings together several interesting characteristics: a small state with global ambitions, a developing country dependent on a single exportable commodity, a Marxist–Leninist regime in the backyard of the United States, a Caribbean nation involved in the anticolonial struggle of post-Spanish rule, and a non-aligned state with special relations with Moscow.

Some American policymakers cast doubts on the scope of Cuban foreign policy. For instance, Henry Kissinger once stated: "It is time that one overcomes the ridiculous myth of the invincible Cubans. Who ever heard of Cubans conducting a global foreign policy?"[1] Other policymakers, like the influential Senator Daniel Patrick Moynihan, distrusted the independence displayed by Cubans in their foreign policy. They saw the Fidelistas only as the "Gurkhas of the Russian Empire,"[2] who functioned as Moscow's front man destabilizing pro-Western Third World states and ultimately aiming to dominate them.

Despite these perceptions, Havana has been an international player of recognized importance, with a good deal of influence among many Third World states. For more traditional students of international politics, the foreign policy of revolutionary Cuba does not fit the prescribed categories of behavior with which they are familiar. Moreover, the paradox about Cuban foreign relations is that Cuba's size and national power do not seem to be consistent with the activity level of its foreign policy. This does not mean "Cuba is a new type of state," as one expert said.[3] Another student of Cuban affairs has more accurately described the Cuban phenomenon as follows: "Cuba is a small country, but it has a big country's foreign policy. It has tried to carry out such a policy since the beginning of the revolution."[4]

You may ask: what motivated Havana to conduct such foreign policy? Perhaps it wanted to apply the "squeaky wheel" principle. By conducting a proactive foreign policy, Revolutionary Cuba attracted global public opinion to itself and, consequently, fought off U.S. influence. These factors led Havana to join the Non-Aligned Movement soon after the revolution. Thus, the main motivations for Cuba's active foreign policy were to protect its revolution and to find a receptive audience for its revolutionary message.

Havana's motives were based on two factors. First is the historical factor, which refers to the extensive U.S. presence in prerevolutionary Cuban economy and politics. This factor is known as the anticolonial trend, which Revolutionary Cuba shares with many members of NAM. The second factor is geographic. Here the issue was how a small island nation could overcome its geographic disadvantage and protect itself vis-à-vis a superpower. The answer was by providing the other superpower with an opportunity to expand its presence and by conducting a highly visible foreign policy in defense of the common concerns of Third World states.

WHY A NON-ALIGNMENT STRATEGY?

Students of international and Cuban affairs have suggested several theories to explain Havana's proactive foreign policy. Some have called this proactive foreign policy "Cuban internationalism,"[5] while others have referred to it as "Cuban globalism."[6] There are also a variety of perspectives on Cuba's decision to join the Non-Aligned Movement. Among the most well-known theories are the surrogate thesis, the convergence of interests approach, the leverage theory, and the natural ally approach.

The Surrogate Thesis

This theory basically suggests that Cuban foreign policy was one element of the grand strategy of Moscow—expansionism. According to this view, the Russians used the opportunity provided by the revolution to penetrate the political structure of Cuba.[7] This was accomplished by using Cuba's economic vulnerability due to its economic dependency on a single commodity—sugar.[8] Using such vulnerability, Moscow created a commercially dependent relationship, which presumably gave it a predominant role in Cuban foreign policymaking[9]. In other words, the advocates of this thesis took some of the main ideas of the dependency theory[10] and applied them to the Havana–Moscow relationship.

A little-known aspect of this thesis is its main assumption that Havana did not initiate an independent foreign relations strategy of its own, but was simply an instrument of someone else's policy. The supporters of this theory have mostly been among the policymakers, like Senators Daniel Patrick Moynihan and John McCain, while its critics have mainly been academicians, like Professors Jorge Dominquez and Martin Weinstein. The latter, for example, suggested, "To see the

Cubans as pawns or mercenaries for the Russians is to deny the history of Cuban solidarity and sacrifice in various areas of the world."[11]

The attraction of this thesis might be that it simplifies the complex international environment for most policymakers and ordinary citizens. Furthermore, it serves to mobilize the typical, unsophisticated citizen for or against a policy. It was also easier to assume that any political advantage a Marxist regime gained was orchestrated by the Soviet Union and implemented by a satellite state against the national security of the United States. In a bipolar structure, the main advantage of this view is that it contributes to the status quo between the two superpowers.

The real world, however, is often more complex. Moreover, not all diplomatic moves are so clear-cut and easily categorized in theoretically sound ways. In fact, the Havana–Moscow relationship is much more sophisticated and complex than portrayed by the surrogate thesis. Doubts about this theory were strengthened by several diverging interests that were developing between revolutionary Cuba and the Soviet Union in Africa and Latin America. In Africa, for instance, the best example happened in Angola. After the Cuban-backed (MPLA) victory, a pro-Soviet faction of MPLA organized a coup against Agostinho Neto in May of 1977. The Soviets did not warn Neto, although they knew about it in advance. Without directly confronting the Soviets, the Cubans joined the MPLA to fight the pro-Soviet faction.[12] Throughout the 1960s in Latin America, the Soviets and Cubans took different positions on how the socialist revolution should be brought to Latin America. Considering Latin America to be in the sphere of American influence, the Soviets took a more cautious approach and hoped that the existing local communist parties would eventually gain power. On the other hand, Revolutionary Cuba was convinced that the Latin American environment was ripe for a socialist revolution and tried to repeat their guerrilla war experience in those countries.[13]

The Convergence of Interests Approach

This approach is founded on the assumption that diplomatic cooperation between states depends on producing mutually beneficial results. Although the national interest of a particular state is uniquely its own, there are also areas of common ground with other states. It is this common ground that provides the basis for cooperation.

In the Havana–Moscow relationship, common ideology played an important role in encouraging cooperative efforts. In fact, ideology is an essential part of Cuban society and public affairs. According to one expert: "Cuba is a curiously ideological country. There is much discussion of ideology. There are particular ways of forming questions, of seeing and understanding the world, that stem from deep ideological convictions that are often well thought-out."[14]

Ideology also contributes significantly to Cuba's solidarity with the developing countries. For instance, the common ground between Cuba and many new Third World states was their colonial past. Havana also shares an international political agenda with most NAM members and supports an international economic plan

(NIEO) to improve the economic development process of the South. As another student of Cuban affairs asserted: "Cuba's solidarity with the less developed tier of nations is an intrinsic element in the political socialization of every Cuban school child. It represents the projection onto the international stage of one of the fundamental strands of Cuba's internal, national ideology."[15] Thus, revolutionary Cuba's interest in Third World affairs was mainly part of its internal political structure and not due to any Soviet pressure.

Based on the convergence of interests approach, even though Havana was an autonomous player, Cuban policy goals also occasionally served Soviet interests. This does not mean that there was a patron–client relationship between the two states. Because of the convergence of their interests, Havana and Moscow considered themselves to be on friendly terms. Friends, however, do not always remain friendly toward each other. Lord Palmerston once declared that states do not have permanent friends or foes, only permanent interests.[16]

Cuba's foreign policy, especially its non-alignment strategy, was not dictated by Moscow. Havana set the tone and intensity of its own foreign relations posture, taking into consideration domestic and international conditions at the time. Nevertheless, this strategy and its goal of promoting ties with many developing countries was quite beneficial to the Russians since Cuba tried to bridge the gap between the socialist camp and the developing world. For instance, the growing influence of Havana among many African nations was the direct result of Havana's intervention on behalf of the anticolonial movements on the continent. This Cuban involvement, which required Soviet assistance, also improved the public image of the Russians in a continent that had historically learned to distrust the intentions of Europeans in general.

Most African states supported the strategy of Revolutionary Cuba, particularly where African national liberation was concerned. In fact, the Organization of African Unity (OAU) applauded the military involvement of Cuba in Africa. At the 1978 meeting in Khartoum, the OAU tacitly approved Cuban military involvement when it did not condemn the presence of Cuban armed forces in Africa. During this meeting, OAU members passed a resolution opposing foreign military bases on the continent, while the organization stated that member states have the right to request foreign military forces [e.g., the Cubans] to protect themselves.[17] Like OAU, NAM also approved the role of Cubans in Africa. In its 1976 summit in Sri Lanka, NAM not only commended Cuba for assisting African nations, it unanimously selected Havana as the site for the 1979 summit.[18] Although the Cubans were involved in different regional conflicts throughout Africa, their most significant military involvement was in Angola, where superpowers were facing one another in a proxy war.[19] One should not forget, however, that Revolutionary Cuba would not have been able to send and supply thousands of troops without the logistic assistance of Moscow, whose interest in this respect complemented those of Havana.[20]

The Leverage Theory

In order to conduct foreign relations based on a non-alignment strategy, one might assume that a developing country would be required to have formal ties with both superpowers. This is not always the case. As mentioned earlier, the non-aligned states are a mixed group whose foreign policies range from pro-West to pro-East. Some of these states, like Cuba, did not even have direct diplomatic contact with the United States. Some others, like Saudi Arabia, had no diplomatic relations with the Soviets, despite Riyadh's active role in the non-aligned meetings and conferences. For the states that had no formal ties with the United States, an indicator of their foreign policy posture toward America was either their ties with American allies, or their foreign relations with the Third World, as is the case for Cuba.[21]

Some experts argued that Cuban foreign relations strategy and its traditional influence among the African, Asian, and Latin American nations within the NAM structure provided Havana with a new sense of leverage in its diplomatic relations. There is evidence to support this view. For instance, the developing world was certainly a source of international support during the sensitive, early days of the 1959 revolution. The Non-Alignment Movement also became a source of political uplift for Revolutionary Cuba, whose bid for leadership finally succeeded when Havana was selected as the site of the 1979 summit. Ties with other non-aligned states also had some economic advantages because Cuba tried to diversify its trade partners to decrease its dependence on the Soviets.

At the time the leadership of NAM and the economic advantages seem to have provided the Cubans with some leverage in dealing with both superpowers. But these two factors were preceded by a change in Havana's foreign policy from a more conflictual to a more conciliatory trend. As Cuba improved its ties with many developing countries, it also eased its security concerns about Washington. And the United States, aiming to improve ties with the Third World, was less willing to jeopardize its policy goal by making any significant moves against Havana.[22]

The increasing political influence of Revolutionary Cuba among many Third World states also changed the nature of Moscow–Havana ties. Cuba became more valuable to the Soviets as Havana established solid ties with many African and Asian capitals. One expert skillfully described the changing nature of Cuban–Russian ties, in which Revolutionary Cuba's proactive foreign policy led to:

> a new sense of leverage in relations with the Soviet Union. The Cuban-Soviet relationship has some unique features when compared with Soviet relations with other East European countries or U.S. relations with other Latin American countries. A superpower has become "dependent" on a little country for some important elements of its foreign policy.[23]

Thus, Havana's enthusiastic support for non-alignment and its energetic participation at NAM conferences, meetings, and summits indicates that Cuban leaders realized the value of active participation in Third World affairs. Havana's political clout grew within the developing world, especially in NAM, as Cuba actively supported Asian and African national liberation movements. Havana's diplomatic prestige also grew as it served as a role model for other Latin American nations to adopt non-aligned foreign relations and to join NAM. The political leverage gained among the developing nations and within NAM soon translated into political leverage against the Great Powers. One can conclude that this sense of leverage provided Havana with comparatively more freedom of action than Soviet allies typically enjoyed.

The Natural Ally Approach

Nevertheless, the leaders of Revolutionary Cuba publicly advocated a very different view of their foreign policy goal, especially of their non-alignment strategy. In this respect, Fidel Castro often made an ideological case for Havana's one-sided non-alignment foreign relations strategy. During international gatherings, Castro often openly stated the socialist path of Revolutionary Cuba. For instance, he began his address to the Fourth Conference of non-aligned states by saying:

> I want to remind you that Cuba is a socialist country, Marxist-Leninist, whose final objective is communism. We are proud of this! On the basis of that concept of human society, we determine our domestic and foreign policies. We are, above all, loyal to the principles of proletarian internationalism, and my words will be consistent with those ideas.[24]

Building on this ideological foundation, Castro envisions a rigid international system portrayed in a black–white or good–evil fashion, similar to the views of other idealogues, like Mao Zedong, President Ronald Reagan, and Ayatollah Khomeini. He defends Cuba's view of non-alignment by adding:

> To our way of thinking, the world is divided into capitalist and socialist countries, imperialist and neocolonized countries, colonialist and colonized countries, reactionary, and progressive countries— governments, in a word, that back imperialism, colonialism, neocolonialism and racism, and governments that oppose imperialism, colonialism, neocolonialism and racism. This seems to us to be basic in the issue of alignment and nonalignment.[25]

Castro rejected other approaches to non-alignment, such as equidistance and two imperialisms. The former is associated with India, while the latter is connected to Revolutionary China, especially after its public split with Moscow. Criticizing those who supported such approaches in conducting their foreign relations strategy, Castro argued:

> The theory of "two imperialisms," one headed by the United States and the other allegedly by the Soviet Union, encouraged by the theoreticians of capitalism, has been echoed at times deliberately and at others through ignorance of history and the

realities of the present-day world, by leaders and spokesmen of nonaligned countries. This is fostered, of course, by those [e.g., China] who regrettably betray the cause of internationalism from supposedly revolutionary positions.[26]

Castro also denies the thesis that American capitalist imperialism and Russian socialist imperialism have equally endangered world peace. He proposed:

How can the Soviet Union be labeled imperialist? ... Where is its participation in multinational companies? What factories, what mines, what oil fields does it own in the underdeveloped world? What worker is exploited in any country of Asia, Africa, or Latin America by Soviet capital?[27]

Focusing on the Cuban historical experience, Castro not only defended the Havana–Moscow alignment, but also encouraged other Third World states to cooperate closely with the socialist camp.[28] The bond between these two worlds, he argued, was their common struggle against the forces of imperialism. Castro emphasized the anticolonial characteristic of the Non-Aligned Movement and its ability to bridge the gap between the developing world and the socialist camp. He concluded that in their common struggle against imperialism, the Third World and Second World states were natural allies, an idea based on Leonid Brezhnev's message to the Fourth Summit.[29] Cuba, however, lost much face among developing countries in the post–1979 era because of its refusal to condemn the Soviet invasion of Afghanistan and its hard sell of the "natural ally" theory to Third World states.

This natural-ally version of non-alignment is rooted in Cuban historical, economic, and political relations with Washington since the Spanish-American War of 1899. Although all Latin American nations have experienced the weight of the American economic presence in different degrees, prerevolutionary Cuba was the most pronounced example of the U.S. presence. This historical factor, plus the geopolitical vulnerability of Cuba in relation to the United States, fed into the socialist ideology of the Cuban elite and the nationalistic feelings of the Cuban masses.

The absence in its history of an unwelcome Soviet presence and the geographic distance between Havana and Moscow allowed Revolutionary Cuba to see the Russians in a different light. In an October 1974 interview with Dan Rather of CBS News, Castro illustrated the contextual differences between the Cuban relations with the two superpowers:

How can our relations with the Soviet Union be compared with the relations that existed with the United States?... The United States owned our mines. The United States was the owner of our electric power plants, of our telephone companies, of the main transportation companies, of the principal industries, of the best lands, of the largest sugar mills. They owned our banks, they owned our foreign trade. In a few words, they owned the Cuban economy. The Soviets do not own a single mine in Cuba, not a single factory, not a single mill, not one hectare of land, not a single bank, not a single business, not a single utility. So then, all the natural resources, all the industries, and all the means of production belong to our country and before the revolution they were under the ownership of another country.[30]

Although the domestic policies of Revolutionary Cuba leave no doubt that the regime in Havana has a strong sense of Marxist–Leninist mission, there is also no doubt that the statement by Castro evinces strong nationalistic sentiments.[31] Knowing this leads us to other scenarios and research questions. For example, did Revolutionary Cuba maintain the same tone and nature of non-alignment in the first decade of the revolution? Would Cuban foreign relations have been very different if Cuba were located elsewhere, like in Central America or even South America? What if the U.S. presence in Cuba were not as profound and extensive?

TRENDS IN CUBAN FOREIGN RELATIONS

The foreign relations of Revolutionary Cuba in the first decade can be categorized into three overlapping periods. The first phase was from January of 1959, when Batista fled, to January of 1962 when the Organization of American States (OAS) suspended Cuban membership. Next was the isolation period that followed the Cuban missile crisis. The third period was triggered by the death of Che Guevara in December of 1967 when Cuban leaders started to show more flexibility in their foreign policy posture.

A Two-Track Policy: 1959–1962

During this period, Cuba pursued two-track foreign relations with the superpowers. One track was oriented toward distancing Havana from Washington, and the other was toward establishing ties with Moscow.[32] Students of Cuban affairs have various explanations for Cuba's foreign relations with the superpowers, with some arguing that American economic and political pressure left no choice for the Cuban leaders other than establishing close ties with the Russians.[33]

Advocating an opposing point of view, some assert that President Castro, a self-declared socialist, had the intention from the beginning of severing Cuba–U.S. ties and taking the country to the Eastern camp.[34] According to this view, Castro's cry for non-alignment was nothing more than a sham and a political cover for his real goal of bringing the whole Non-Alignment Movement closer to the Soviet position. Finally, there are others who analyze Cuban foreign relations from a nationalistic perspective.[35]

Although each group makes interesting points, they all seem to take a rather deterministic approach in explaining Cuba's ties with the superpowers. I believe, however, that neither did the Cuban leaders have a preset scenario, nor were there extraordinary forces that directed the leaders of Havana, Moscow, or Washington toward certain political choices. I also do not believe in a conspiracy theory against

President Fidel Castro of Cuba visited the UN several times and addressed the General Assembly as shown above. He has successfully used the diplomatic channels in the UN system to neutralize the political pressure of the West, especially Washington. *Photograph courtesy of UN/DPI Photo.*

the national interest of the United States or Cuba. The prudent method of studying Cuban foreign relations is to analyze with impartiality how certain events and issues contributed to the formation of Cuban foreign policy.

The first period of Cuban non-alignment strategy began with the triumph of the revolution when the rebel army troops under Ernesto Che Guevara entered Havana on 1 January 1959. Fidel Castro, the commander of the rebel army, soon became prime minister of the revolutionary government. In April of 1959, Castro made a highly publicized trip to the United States at the invitation of the Association of Newspaper Editors. During this visit he also met with Vice-President Richard Nixon, who was not impressed with Castro despite the media's mostly positive image of this young upper-class-lawyer-*cum*-rebel.[36]

The first controversy in American–Cuban relations came when the issue of compensation for the expropriation of U.S.-owned assets was raised after Revolutionary Cuba passed the 1959 Agrarian Reform Law, which nationalized about one-third of the arable land on the island. Earlier in 1959 the Eisenhower administration did not have a policy in place if Revolutionary Cuba began to nationalize American property, mainly because there were voices in the administration suggesting restraint.[37] By mid–1959, however, the advocates of accommodation were gone and the administration had a clearly antagonistic posture toward Cuba. An indicator of the administration's sentiment toward Cuba was Eisenhower's leaving for a golfing trip to Georgia during Castro's visit.[38] In February of 1960, Washington became alarmed when Soviet Foreign Minister Anastas Mikoyan visited Cuba and signed trade and aid agreements. After this visit, momentum in Cuban–Soviet relations built steadily from 1960 to 1962.[39] When Havana and Moscow formally established diplomatic relations in May, the Eisenhower administration became concerned that the Soviets had found a foothold in the Western hemisphere—only ninety miles from U.S. shores.

From mid–1960, there was an upsurge in conflictual behavior between Washington and Havana, with Moscow being the beneficiary of this quarrel.[40] In June, the U.S. State Department urged American oil companies to refuse to refine Soviet crude oil at their Cuban refineries. In response, Revolutionary Cuba decided to nationalize those refineries. After this tit-for-tat exchange, Cuban–American ties soon degenerated into a cycle of economic retribution as each state tried to outdo the other in flexing its muscles.[41] In July, the United States suspended the Cuban sugar quota that affected approximately 80 percent of Cuba's exports to the United States. Although Havana found a new customer—the Russians—for the sugar refused by the Americans, it retaliated in August by nationalizing $1 billion worth of American private investment on the island. By the end of the month, Washington retaliated and imposed an embargo on trade with Cuba. In mid October, Havana nationalized all large commercial and industrial enterprises.

Contrary to popular belief, these bold decisions of the revolutionary idealists, like Fidel and Raul Castro and Che Guevara, did not please the Soviets. In fact, Moscow was unsure about the ideological convictions of the top leaders of the 26 July Movement—the Fidelistas—because they had not given any significant role to the well-established Communist party of Cuba (the Popular Socialist party, or PSP).[42] The latter was concerned that the actions of the revolutionary idealists would provoke American military intervention that would put the Soviets in a difficult political position—that of having to defend Cuba and take the risk of a global confrontation with the United States, or that of potentially allowing the socialist regime in Cuba to be dissipated by American intervention.[43]

The gap between Havana and Washington continued to widen. The United States broke off diplomatic relations with Cuba on 3 January 1961. Three months later, Castro declared that the Cuban Revolution was socialist.[44] According to Raul Castro, a revolutionary idealist, this meant that the revolution had passed the liberation phase and entered the construction of socialism phase.[45] It also meant that idealists had consolidated their power in setting both domestic and foreign policy agendas.

Shortly thereafter, the failure of the Bay of Pigs invasion not only created diplomatic embarrassment for the United States, but contributed to Castro's solidification of the government and the increased global attention paid to the Cuban's anticolonial cry at international gatherings. For example, Revolutionary Cuba was the only Latin American state represented at the founding conference of NAM. In reference to Cuba's case, the non-aligned countries stated in Article 13 of the Belgrade Declaration of 1961: "The participating countries believe that the right of Cuba, as that of any other nation to freely choose their political and social systems in accordance with their own conditions, needs and possibilities, should be respected."[46] Obviously, the diplomatic publicity that Havana gained from such global support created an environment with a psychological edge for the young revolutionary regime. One expert concluded, "Clearly, Cuba's active participation in the non-alignment movement was very beneficial to her."[47]

By 2 December, relations between the United States and Cuba had deteriorated to such a degree that Castro did not think he had much to lose by declaring, "I am a Marxist-Leninist and I shall be one to the end of my life."[48] This statement was also an indicator that the revolution was quite secure at home and that the revolutionary idealists had carefully dominated the formulation and implementation of foreign policy.

The Isolation Years: 1962–1967

Many experts often view the Cuban missile crisis as a turning point in the diplomatic history of Cuba, but the image of the revolutionary Cuban leadership was changing even before the October crisis began.[49] In fact, Castro's declaration of his Marxist orientation had already turned off some Western educated Third World leaders who had previously thought of Castro as a nationalistic leader fighting American colonialism in a David versus Goliath scenario. One expert argued that the Cubans' ideological tone "had relegated them to the fringes of the Non-aligned Movement and Third World affairs."[50] At that time Cuba had not yet established close ties with most non-aligned states. Its participation at the NAM meeting was basically a public relations effort to gain political support for Cuban grievances against the United States. Moreover, the revolutionary idealists in Havana were more interested in exporting their revolution, contacting liberation movements, and supporting Marxist opposition in other countries than in conducting foreign policy through ordinary government-to-government relations.

In Latin America, where Cuba was the only NAM member, some leaders began to suspect the real intention of the revolutionary Cubans who supported attempts to export Cuban-style revolutions. Although some maintained that these attempts in the 1960s were largely defensive in nature,[51] Havana's efforts made it easier for the United States to launch the Alliance for Progress and lead OAS to suspend Cuba's membership in the organization by January of 1962.[52] The Second Declaration of Havana in February was in response to this decision of OAS and it signaled the start of a Cuban call for armed struggle. In this declaration, Castro called upon all Latin Americans to stand firmly against the forces of colonialism and to remember that "the duty of a revolutionary is to make the revolution." This declaration clearly illustrates the idealism that permeated the political culture of Revolutionary Cuba during the isolation years.[53]

In October of 1962, intermediate-range ballistic missiles provided to Revolutionary Cuba by the Soviet Union triggered the Cuban missile crisis, which is often noted not only for its significance in the relations between the two superpowers, but also as the incident that shattered the hopes for improved U.S.–Cuba ties. Many, however, fail to recognize that this incident also dampened Cuban–Soviet relations, mainly because the Soviets acted without consulting Cuba.[54] During the isolation years, Havana was not only alienated from the United States, but it was also disenchanted with the policy priorities of the Soviet Union.[55] This disenchantment led to the development of an independent foreign policy.[56]

The aggressive attempts to export a Cuban-style revolution throughout Latin America by means of guerrilla tactics had two results. First, all member states of OAS except Mexico voted to break diplomatic and economic ties with Cuba on 26 July 1964. Second, Soviet–Cuban relations deteriorated rapidly because Havana's strategy of creating small guerrilla *foco* groups conflicted with Moscow's strategy of working through the established Latin American leftist parties.[57] Castro, however, continued to aid guerrilla movements in Venezuela, Colombia, Peru, Guatemala, and the Caribbean.[58]

The revolutionary idealists put a conflictual tone on Cuban foreign policy in the mid–1960s. In 1965, Che Guevara, the most prominent revolutionary idealist, left Havana with a mandate to wage armed struggles in Africa and Latin America but to avoid direct involvement by Cuba in the domestic affairs of other states. In January of the next year, Havana hosted the first Tricontinental Congress, which formed the Organization of Solidarity with the Peoples of Africa, Asia, and Latin America (OSPAAAL), which in turn organized a united front of liberation movements across three continents. Also during this conference, the delegates representing all Latin American nations (including Puerto Rico, Trinidad and Tobago) established the Latin America Solidarity Organization (OLAS). For

Havana, the latter was a policy instrument free of Moscow's influence for implementing the vision of Cuban revolutionary idealists.[59] In July of 1967, OLAS held its first conference in Cuba. The conference concluded that guerrilla struggle was the fundamental path to Latin American revolution. This conclusion was far from the Soviet position, although it was closer to the Chinese position on the exporting of revolution. Havana's aggressive, direct, and independent foreign relations moves toward Third World states brought Soviet–Cuban tensions to a head. According to one student of Cuban affairs, Cuba and the Soviet Union learned to work together to organize OSPAAAL in January of 1966, but for different reasons.[60]

Throughout the isolation era, U.S.–Cuban relations remained tense and conflictual. In December of 1966, a U.S. Air Force pilot was shot down over Cuba and captured after dropping arms and equipment intended for an anti-Castro group. One expert maintained that U.S. support for anti-Castro groups continued until 1966.[61] The revolutionary idealists hoped to see the United States pinned down in several Vietnam-style conflicts in Latin America so U.S. attention would be diverted from Cuba. For example, on 16 April 1967 Che Guevara sent a message to the second Tricontinental Congress, calling for the creation of "two, three, many Vietnams." Meanwhile Havana continued to actively export revolution. For instance, on 12 May 1967 twelve men, including four Cubans, were intercepted by Venezuelan troops as they landed on a remote Venezuelan beach. This tactic was reminiscent of the 26 July movement in prerevolutionary Cuba. Nevertheless, the Soviet Union and Cuba disagreed about the policy instruments that were supposed to bring socialist-style revolution to Latin America, particularly in Venezuela and Colombia. While the cautious Russians pushed for normalization of relations with these states and working through their local communist parties, the impatient Cubans had designated them as targets of guerrilla warfare.[62]

Thus, Cuban foreign relations based on a non-alignment strategy with both superpowers can be defined as aggressive and uncompromising in the isolation period. This is not to suggest that Havana treated both Washington and Moscow equally. It was obvious that the United States faced Cuban aggressive and uncompromising policy much more than their Soviet counterparts. However, the context and conduct of Cuban foreign relations and its non-alignment strategy began to change as early as 1968.

A Conciliatory Posture: 1968–1969

On 9 October 1967, the murder of Che Guevara in the Bolivian village of Vallegrande shocked the revolutionary idealists in Havana. Bolivia, where a military regime led the poorest state in South America,[63] was the main target of those Cuban revolutionary idealists who foresaw the domestic conditions of the country to be best suited for a Cuban style revolution. They failed to realize that there were more differences than similarities between prerevolutionary Cuba and Bolivia. When Che Guevara was killed at the hands of Bolivian rangers, they reevaluated the whole *foco* theory of revolution.[64] A comparison between the two states showed differences in the levels of rural support for the rebels, the topography, and the ethnic features of the target state. The death of Che Guevara marked the failure and end of *foco* tactics.

In January of 1968, Cuban leaders learned another valuable lesson. A cutback in deliveries of crude oil from the Soviet Union forced Havana to introduce gasoline rationing. The cutback seemed to shock some of the top revolutionary leaders, who were already facing difficult decisions since the Cuban economy performed poorly in the late 1960s. Soon Castro declared that "the dignity of the Revolution demanded that Cubans refrain from begging for additional supplies from the Soviet Union."[65] The lesson learned was clear—Revolutionary Cuba was still an economically dependent state.

This realization and the poor performance of the economy[66] contributed to a significant conciliatory gesture of Cuba toward the Soviets. On 23 August 1968, Castro supported the Soviet invasion of Czechoslovakia.[67] He called the Warsaw Pact nations' invasion a "drastic and painful measure" but a "bitter necessity." He also declared that it "saved" socialism in Czechoslovakia and criticized the Czech Communist party for its "bureaucratic methods of leadership." From Havana's perspective, interestingly enough, the intervention was a sign of reassurance for being able to count on Soviet aid during an emergency rather than a threat to their national security. This view was based on the principle of the irreversibility of the socialist revolution and the willingness of the cautious Soviet leaders to risk international crisis to "save" Czechoslovakia.[68]

Although Cuba's approval of the invasion of Czechoslovakia has been interpreted by some as evidence for the so-called surrogate thesis, Castro was willing to pay the price for several political advantages of this move. First, Havana's diplomatic support for Moscow was crucial at the time and was considered a favor in return for Soviet aid. The 1968 invasion elicited not only criticism in the West over the Soviets' willingness to use force, but also raised concerns in some capitals of the Eastern camp—notably Beijing—over their own security and degree of independence from Moscow. At this time, the Soviets needed any diplomatic support that they received, so they appreciated the Cuban effort.

Second, the Sino–Soviet split provided Cuba with an opportunity to take the place of China and perhaps gain access to some of the Soviet resources at the disposal of the Chinese.[69] Third, its geographic position provided Havana with the luxury of supporting a Soviet invasion of a European or Asian state. Havana itself had virtually no fear of a Soviet invasion since it was located at a safe distance and was valuable to the Soviet Union due to its central location in the New World. Fourth, in his statement supporting the invasion, Castro seized the opportunity to criticize once again the "bureaucratic" nature and methods of the typical Eastern European communist parties. The role of these so-called bureaucratic structures to promote socialist revolutions abroad was a controversial issue and a major difference between Moscow and Havana, as mentioned earlier. In fact, one expert concentrated on such differences by describing the uneasy relationship of a typical Latin American leftist party with a rebel like Castro.[70] Fifth, the impatient Castro put his seal of approval on the use of force to promote socialism. This was not a deviation from his previous position.

During this period, Cuba's increasing and direct economic dependence on the Soviet Union and its poor economic performance preoccupied the minds of top leaders. To break this psychological barrier, the revolutionary idealists mobilized Cuba in May of 1969 for a sugar harvest of 10 million tons, the largest in Cuban history.[71] By December of the next year, however, Castro acknowledged the failure to meet this goal. The attempt caused the most serious economic and political dislocation in the modern history of Cuba. The failure to meet this goal (like the death of Che Guevara and the realization of economic dependency on the Soviets) had a humbling effect on the revolutionary spirit of the young idealistic Cuban leaders and amplified the concerns of the more pragmatic leaders. The latter realized that great devotion to the cause and great striving are required, but do not guarantee success. As I indicated in the previous chapter, the Chinese revolutionary idealists learned a similar lesson during the Korean War.

The economic difficulties contributed to the emergence of more realistic leaders, like Carlos Rafael Rodriguez. He was among a group of more pragmatic "old communists" from PSP and the new generation of technocratic managers. Rodriguez rose in the ranks of leadership, gained more power in the decision-making apparatus, and consequently imposed greater constraints on the more idealistic Fidelistas. He served as minister without portfolio for years and was appointed as the chairman of Cuba's delegation to the Intergovernmental Soviet–Cuban Commission for Economic, Scientific, and Technological Cooperation. Soon he became Deputy Prime Minister in Charge of Foreign Economic and Diplomatic Relations. Later, he was even granted membership in the Political Bureau of the Communist Party of Cuba (PCC), established by the Fidelistas.[72] As one expert indicated:

> The impulse toward greater pragmatism on the economic, political, and diplomatic fronts reflects the new influence of the civilian technocratic and managerial elite. It also stems from the greater Soviet involvement in Cuban affairs since 1970 which, in turn, has reinforced the position of the more pragmatic leadership within Cuba.[73]

High on the agenda of the revolutionary realists was economic development, which had not received much attention from the Fidelistas in favor of a proactive foreign policy. The realists also supported "greater trade and technological ties with the advanced countries of the socialist and non-socialist worlds."[74] Many revolutionary realists, particularly Rodriguez, advocated improving U.S.–Cuba relations, mainly because "a whole range of technologies was not yet available in the socialist camp."[75] By improving relations with the United States, the realists hoped to obtain American agricultural equipment, technology, computer facilities, and so on.[76]

All these developments led to a change in the Cuban foreign relations strategy from conflictual, isolationist, and anti-status quo (advocated by the more idealistic individuals) to a more conciliatory and cooperative posture (supported by the more realistic leaders). The first target of this more conciliatory policy was the Eastern camp states. Courted by his more pragmatic comrades, Castro accepted the doctrine of "many roads to socialism," which was an attempt to show more flexibility in his approach and promised more solidarity with the socialist camp. In July of 1969, seven Russian ships visited Cuban ports as a show of solidarity between Havana and Moscow.

To build a larger network of friendly states, Revolutionary Cuba relaxed its criteria for defining its friends. This was mostly done by "placing greater weight on anti-imperialistic credentials than ideological beliefs."[77] This meant that Havana showed more tolerance for the political choices made by other developing countries and non-aligned states. Cuban non-alignment strategy also exhibited signs of flexibility. In this respect, Havana gave a cooperative diplomatic signal to Washington by making the arrangements for the arrival of the first contingent of the Vencerenos Brigade, a group of volunteer workers from the United States who came to work on the sugar harvest. In general, as one expert suggested "Cuba reverted to its early 1960s policy of seeking normalized government-to-government relations."[78]

These events were the precursors of more profound diplomatic moves by Revolutionary Cuba in the early 1970s. The latter is used by most experts to identify a shift in Cuban foreign affairs. Among the most important developments indicating a change in Cuban strategy in the early 1970's were Castro's sixty-three-day tour of Africa and Eastern Europe in May of 1972, the restoration of diplomatic relations with many Latin American states, an anti-hijacking agreement with the United States in February of 1973, the arrival of U.S. Senators Claiborne Pell and Jacob Javits for an official visit in September of 1974, Secretary Henry Kissinger's acknowledgment on 1 March 1975 that the United States was "prepared to move in a new direction" in its policy toward Cuba, and the OAS decision in July of 1975 to lift diplomatic and economic sanctions against Havana. All of these political developments happened during the more conciliatory period of Cuban foreign relations—in the second decade of the life of Revolutionary Cuba. A detailed analysis of these such developments is beyond the scope of this study: it is sufficient only to point out that they took place.

CONCLUSION

Cuban non-alignment foreign relations strategy was quite beneficial for Havana in the first decade of the revolution, despite the unbalanced ties that Cuba maintained with the two superpowers. It guaranteed the survival of the socialist-style revolution by taking Cuba outside of the regional dominance of the United States. The Cuban leaders, however, did not perceive that they had replaced their historical dependence on the Americans with a new dependence on the Russians because Moscow's presence in Cuba was indirect and not as apparent, even though Russian aid and trade were significant to Cuba.

Havana did not, however, become a totally helpless pawn in the hands of Moscow. The Cuban leaders had played a high stakes game and had made some costly decisions, including Havana's insistence on the adoption of the natural ally approach, Cuba's diplomatic approval of the Soviet invasion of Czechoslovakia, and its refusal to condemn the Soviet invasion of Afghanistan, as explained earlier. Nevertheless, revolutionary Cubans had made their country valuable for a geographically distant superpower that shared their ideological cause.

Cuban non-aligned foreign relations were not static in the first decade of the revolution. There was an upsurge in Cuban-Soviet ties during the first years of the revolutionary regime. They then took a downturn after the missile crisis when the Cubans felt betrayed by their ideological partners. In the isolation years, Cuban leaders disagreed with the Soviet policy in Latin American and had no direct relations with the United States.

The failure of the *foco* tactic to export revolution and the economic shortcomings of the regime finally provided an opportunity in the late 1960s for the revolutionary realists to push for more pragmatic economic plans. The latter required not only an institutional change,[79] but also a more conciliatory foreign policy. Thus, 1968 and 1969 were the beginning of an era of generally improving relations with the Great Powers and many developing countries. This task was accomplished by downplaying the differences and emphasizing the similarities in domestic economic challenges and foreign policy goals.

Obviously, this study has indicated some similarities between the motives and means of foreign policies of revolutionary Cuba and China. There have also been similarities in the trends of their non-alignment strategies with the superpowers. There is, however, the possibility that the similarity of the behavior of these two states is due to coincidence and that there are no particular patterns of behavior for these revolutionary states. We can put such skepticism to rest by analyzing the diplomatic relations of Revolutionary Iran.

NOTES

1. "Castro: Russia's Cat's Paw," *Newsweek* (12 June 1978).

2. This phrase is quoted in "Castro's Globetrotting Gurkhas," *Time* (23 February 1976), 25.

3. Mark Falcoff, "Cuba: Thirty Years of a Revolutionary Foreign Policy," in *The Cuban Revolution at Thirty*, Occasional Paper No. 29 (Washington, D.C.: The Cuban American National Foundation, January 1989), 53.

4. Jorge I. Dominguez, "Cuban Foreign Policy," *Foreign Affairs* vol. 57 (Fall 1978): 83.

5. See William M. LeoGrande, "Foreign Policy: The Limits of Success," *Cuba: Internal and International Affairs* ed. Jorge I. Dominguez (Beverly Hills, Calif.: Sage, 1982), 167-92.

6. See H. Michael Erisman, *Cuba's International Relations* (Boulder, Colo.: Westview Press, 1985), especially chapters 3-5.

7. For some original thinking on the concept of a penetrated political system, see James Rosenau, "Pre-Theories and Theories of Foreign Policy," *Approaches to Comparative and International Politics* ed. R. Barry Farrell (Evanston, Ill.: Northwestern University Press, 1966), 63-71. For a concise and updated review of the concept penetration" see John T. Rourke, *International Politics on the World Stage*, 3d ed. (Guilford, Conn.: Dushkin Publishing Group, Inc., 1991), 295-320.

8. On the Cuban sugar industry, see G. B. Hagelberg, "Cuba's Sugar Policy," in *Revolutionary Cuba in the World Arena*, ed. Martin Weinstein (Philadelphia: Institute for the Study of Human Issues, 1979), 31-50; also see Jorge F. Perez-Lopez, "Sugar and Petroleum in Cuban-Soviet Terms of Trade," in *Cuba in the World*, eds. Cole Blasier and Carmelo Mesa-Lago (Pittsburgh: University of Pittsburgh Press, 1979).

9. The main aspects of Havana's dependence on Moscow are illustrated in Jiri Valenta, "The Soviet-Cuban Alliance in Africa and the Caribbean," *World Today* (February 1981): 46-7.

10. This theory was first suggested by those Third World scholars interested in the process of economic and political development. For example, see Fernando H. Cardoso, "Associated-Dependent Development: Theoretical and Practical Implications," in *Authoritarian Brazil: Origins, Policies, and Future*, ed. Alfred Stepan (New Haven, Conn.: Yale University Press, 1973); Theotonio dos Santos, "The Structure of Dependence," *The American Economic Review* 60, no. 2 (May 1970): 231-36; J. Samuel Valenzuela and Arturo Valenzuela, "Modernization and Dependency: Alternative Perspectives in the Study of Latin American Underdevelopment," *Comparative Politics* 10, no. 2 (July 1978): 535-57.

11. Weinstein, 4; for criticism of the surrogate thesis based on Cuban involvement overseas, see Jorge I. Dominguez, "Cuban Military and National Security Policies," in Weinstein, 77-97.

12. See William LeoGrande, "Cuban-Soviet Relations and Cuban Policy in Africa," paper presented at the 1979 convention of the International Studies Association (Toronto, Canada), p. 27; Gerald J. Bender, "Angola, the Cubans, and American Anxieties," *Foreign Policy* no. 31 (Spring 1978): 26; *New York Times* (14 December 1978): A14; and Nelson P. Valdes, "The Evolution of Cuban Foreign Policy in Africa," paper presented at the 1979 convention of the International Studies Association (Toronto, Canada), p. 71.

13. For an explanation of the conflicting Soviet and Cuban positions on a wide range of ideological issues, see chapters 2 and 3 in Jacques Levesque, *The U.S.S.R. and the Cuban Revolution* (New York: Praeger Special Series, 1978).

14. Dominguez, *Internal and International Affairs*, 14.

15. Nita Rous Manitzas, "Cuban Ideology and Nationhood: Their Meaning in the Americas," in Weinstein, 139.

16. Cited in Erisman, 10.

17. *New York Times*, 26 July 1978, p. 5: *Facts on File* 38, no. 1968 (28 July 1978): 561.

18. Stated in William LeoGrande, "Evolution of the Nonaligned Movement," *Problems of Communism* 19 (January-February 1980): 43.

19. On Cuban foreign policy motives in Angola, see Abraham F. Lowenthal, "Why Cuba Is in Angola," in Weinstein, 99-107.

20. On the role of the Soviets and Cubans in turning the tide to the advantage of MPLA during the war in Angola, see Daniel Fogel, *Africa In Struggle: National Liberation and Proletarian Revolution*, 2d ed, (San Francisco: Ism Press, 1986), 242-44.

21. On this subject also see Erisman, 31-35.

22. Ibid., 6.

23. Jorge I. Dominguez, "The Success of Cuban Foreign Policy," *New York University Occasional Papers* 27 (January 1980): 6.

24. Fidel Castro's speech at the Fourth Conference of Non-Aligned Nations, Algiers, 7 September 1973. The full text was printed in *Granma Weekly Review*, 16 September 1973.

25. Ibid.

26. Castor's address, the Fourth Conference of Non-Aligned nations.

27. Ibid.

28. Erisman, 47.

29. Erisman, 48.

30. *CBS Reports*, "Castro, Cuba, and the USA," (22 October 1974). Also quoted in Weinstein, 147-48.

31. On the impact of nationalism on the Cuban society and foreign policy, see Erisman.

32. For a concise summary of Havana's making of the revolution phase, see Thomas C. Wright, *Latin America in the Era of the Cuban Revolution* (New York: Praeger, 1991), 21-39.

33. William M. LeoGrande, 168. Also see, Philip Brenner, *From Confrontation to Negotiation: U.S. Relations with Cuba* (Boulder, Colo.: Westview Press, 1988).

34. Hugh S. Thomas, George A. Fauriol, and Juan Carlos Weiss, *The Cuban Revolution Twenty Five Years Later* (Boulder, Colo.: Westview Press, 1984), especially pp. 3-4.

35. For example, see Erisman, especially pp. 9-11.

36. Hugh S. Thomas, 2.

37. For example, see Philip Bonsal, *Cuba, Castro and the United States* (Pittsburgh: University of Pittsburgh Press, 1971).

38. See Herbert L. Matthews, *Revolution in Cuba* (New York: Scribner's, 1975), chapters 6-8.

39. For a clear and concise summary of the dynamics of Cuban–Soviet ties in the early years, see Levesque, 3-25.

40. For an analysis of the role of the Soviets in the U.S.–Cuban conflict, see Cole Blasier, "The Soviet Union in the Cuban-American Conflict," in Blasier and Mesa-Lago, 37-52.

41. See Jorge I. Dominguez, *Cuba: Order and Revolution* (Cambridge: Harvard University Press, Belknap Press, 1978), 144-48.

42. Erisman, 17.

43. Daniel Tretiak, *Perspectives on Cuba's Relations with the Communist System* (Ann Arbor, Mich.: Xerox University Microfilms, 1975), 120-21.

44. Peter Wyden, *Bay of Pigs: The Untold Story* (New York: Simon and Schuster, 1979), 185.

45. Levesque, 30.

46. *Medjunarodna Politika* [Belgrade, Yugoslavia] 15, no. 348 (5 October 1964): 8-12.

47. Rozita Levi, "Cuba and the Non-aligned Movement," in Blasier and Mesa-Lago, 149.

48. Quoted in Thomas L. Karnes, ed., *Readings in the Latin American Policy of the United States* (Tucson: University of Arizona Press, 1972), 280.

49. Among the better known books on the missile crisis are Graham T. Allison, *Essence of Decision* (Boston: Little, Brown, 1971), which is a fine example of crisis analysis from an academic point of view.; Robert F. Kennedy, *Thirteen Days: A Memoir of the Cuban Missile Crisis* (New York: W. W. Norton, 1969), which gives the perspective of an insider policymaker; K. S. Karol, *Guerrillas in Power: The Course of the Cuban Revolution* (New

York: Hill and Wang, 1970), which is perhaps the best treatment of the crisis from Havana's point of view, especially pp. 249-81.

50. Erisman, 31.

51. For example, see LeoGrande, 170.

52. For a more comprehensive account, see Gordon Connell-Smith, *The Inter-American System* (New York: Oxford University Press, 1966), especially pp. 250-53 and 176-80. Also, notice that Brenner places the isolation of Cuba as the America's second foreign policy goal toward Havana during the 1959–1971 period, just behind the overthrow of Castro (see Brenner, 17).

53. The full text of the Second Declaration is in Martin Kenner and James Petras, eds., *Fidel Castro Speaks* (New York: Grove Press, 1969), 85-106.

54. Tad Szulc, *Fidel: A Critical Portrait* (New York: Morrow, 1986), 585.

55. Among the better studies showing different points of friction between Havana and Moscow are John McShane, "Small States in the International System: A Cuban Case Study," paper presented at the 1979 Convention of the Southeastern Council on Latin American Studies, Tampa, Florida; William Durch, "The Cuban Military in Africa and the Middle East: From Algeria to Angola," *Studies in Comparative Communism* 11 (Spring/Summer 1978): 37-41.

56. For example, see Tretiak.

57. On the goal and failure of the *foco* tactic, see George Fauriol, ed., *Latin American Insurgencies* (Washington, D.C.: National Defense University Press, 1985), 132-35.

58. For a detailed explanation of Cuban efforts to export its revolution see Wright, chapters 3-6.

59. Erisman, 31. For details about OLAS's nature and purpose, see John Gerassi, "Havana: A New International is Born," in *Latin American Radicalism*, eds. Irving Horowitz, Josue DeCastro, and John Gerassi (New York: Random House, 1969), 532-42; and Castro's keynote speech to the founding conference, "Waves of the Future," ibid., 543-79. For a detailed explanation of Cuban efforts to export its revolution, see Wright, chapters 3-6.

60. Erisman, 30.

61. Brenner, 16.

62. Eugenio Hernandez, *Cuban-Soviet Relations: Divergence and Convergence*, Occasional Paper No. 3, (Washington, D.C.: Latin American Studies Program, Georgetown University, 1980), 8.

63. For an excellent summary of the Bolivian political climate, see Eduardo A. Gamarra and James M. Malloy, "Bolivia: Revolution and Reaction," in *Latin American Politics and Development*, 3d eds. Howard J. Wiarda and Harvey F. Kline (Boulder, Colo.: Westview Press, 1990), 359-77.

64. On Cuba's reevaluation of the "export of revolution" strategy, see D. Bruce Jackson, *Castro, the Kremlin, and Communism in Latin America* (Baltimore, Md.: Johns Hopkins University Press, 1969).

65. Brenner, 100.

66. For criticism of the record of Cuban economic development in this period, see Thomas, 20-35. For an analysis of the problems associated with the Cuban economy at the time, see Claes Brundenius, *Revolutionary Cuba: The Challenge of Economic Growth with Equity* (Boulder, Colo.: Westview Press, 1984), 41-104.

67. Erisman, 35.

68. LeoGrande, 6.

69. Tretiak, 128.

70. For example see Erisman, 27.

71. On the significance of the sugar and oil trade in Havana–Moscow ties, see Jorge F. Perez-Lopez, "Sugar and Petroleum in Cuban-Soviet Terms of Trade," in Blasier and Mesa-Lago, 273-99.

72. Edward Gonzalez, "Institutionalization, Political Elites, and Foreign Policies," in Blasier and Mesa-Lago, 3-36, especially see pp. 6-7.

73. Gonzalez, 15.

74. Ibid., 18.

75. *Le Monde*, 16 January 1975. Also cited in Gonzalez, 18.

76. Gonzalez, 19.

77. Erisman, 33.

78. Ibid., 34.

79. These institutional changes followed the constitutional reforms of the mid 1970s; see Gonzalez, 5-16; also see Jorge Dominguez, "Revolutionary Politics: The New Demands for Orderliness," in Dominguez, *Internal and International Affairs*, 19-70.

5

IRANIAN FOREIGN RELATIONS, 1979–1989

From its early days, the revolutionary government declared that Tehran would pursue a policy of non-alignment. In 1979, Iran abandoned The Central Treaty Organization (CENTO) that was founded in 1959.[1] Soon thereafter, Iran joined NAM. It also cancelled many weapons orders from the West, particularly the United States. The assumption of the revolutionary regime was that non-alignment would meet the foreign policy goals of Iran as a Third World state, whereas an alliance with the East or the West would not fit in with Iranian religious, cultural, or historical characteristics. Moreover, an alliance with one of the Great Powers would potentially restrict Iranian policy options in establishing and maintaining mutually beneficial ties with states from the opposing bloc as well as with some Third World states.

From this perspective, the non-alignment of Revolutionary Iran is a new chapter in the history of an ancient country that gained ideological momentum as a result of the 1979 Islamic revolution. Some experts, however, have discounted the effects of revolutionary Islam on Iranian foreign relations by emphasizing geopolitical, historical, and economic factors. They conclude that Tehran's new foreign relations strategy is neither original nor radical.[2] In response to these experts, one could argue that Iran was not a founding member of NAM, and the strategies of Tehran in the pre- and postrevolutionary eras have shown some similarities. Nevertheless, Revolutionary Iran is structurally different from Imperial Iran, and Tehran's declaration of non-alignment was a radical move, challenging the status quo in the strategically significant Persian Gulf region.

ELEMENTS OF IRANIAN FOREIGN POLICY

Before analyzing the elements of Iranian foreign policy, let us first focus on Tehran's objectives for declaring non-alignment. Briefly, Revolutionary Iran had four major goals: achieving autonomy in foreign policymaking, avoiding direct involvement in the American–Russian rivalry, ending Iran's dependence on only one ideological camp, and improving its ties with all nations, except for Israel and the Former South African regime. These Iranian goals were rooted in Iranian history, geopolitics, and economy. The influence of these factors dates to the nineteenth century when the rivalry among the Europeans in the region began. Nevertheless, the condition of Iran under the Shah was the prominent factor in shaping postrevolutionary foreign policy.

Regime stability dominated the Shah's domestic and foreign policies following the 1953 coup that ousted Premier Mohammed Mossadegh.[3] Pursuit of stability created a vicious cycle which ended in Imperial Iran's relying more on foreign powers. Namely, it required an alliance with the United States, which fostered a public image of military and economic dependence on the United States[4] This public image was not necessarily accurate. Trade statistics indicate that Western Europe and Japan were more significant trade partners than the United States.[5] Emphasizing such images, however, Ayatollah Khomeini characterized the Shah as a weak, illegitimate, and dependent leader. Interestingly enough, when the Shah gave some ground to his opposition as a concession to the Carter administration, many Iranians became convinced that the Ayatollah was correct in saying that the Shah was dependent on America. This perception ultimately resulted in weakening the regime both psychologically and politically.

In sum, Iran's revolutionary leaders decided to pursue a non-alignment strategy mainly because they asserted that dependency, a trademark of the Shah's regime, was culturally an anti-Islamic and anti-Iranian notion.

Definitional Problems of Iranian Non-Alignment

Much has been said about the nature of Iranian foreign relations, but ambiguities persist regarding Tehran's definition of non-alignment. For Muhammad Mokri, Revolutionary Iran's first ambassador to Moscow, non-alignment simply meant refusing to join an offensive pact.[6] This definition is vague, considering that NAM criteria allows membership in some military pacts. The question arises: Would Tehran join a defensive pact? Contrary to this rather passive interpretation of non-alignment, Ayatollah Mossavi Ardabili emphasized the active and conflictual characteristics of non-alignment. He pointed out that Islam encompasses attributes opposed to both sides.[7] Minister Ali Akbar Velayati defined non-alignment as maintaining independence from the two blocs and the consequent negation of foreign sovereignty in all aspects.[8]

Ayatollah Khomeini, a strong advocate of a non-aligned strategy, did not offer a clear definition either. Instead, he referred to a popular slogan regarding the meaning of non-alignment: "Neither East nor West, [only] an Islamic Republic."[9]

An Analytical Definition

The phrase "neither East nor West, [only] an Islamic Republic" consists of two parts. The first part negates external elements: the East and the West. It is a denial of formal or informal linkage, namely alignment, with either the East or the West. This leads to the independent position taken by Iran in the policymaking and implementing process. In this respect, Iranian non-alignment is similar to that of other NAM states, especially the revolutionary regimes.

The second part refers to a specific type of regime—[only] an Islamic Republic. This is the unique aspect of Iranian non-alignment policy for two reasons. First, Tehran's definition is not secular like that of other developing countries. Second, it implies a universalization based on one type of regime: a republic based on Islamic values, particularly from the Shia Muslim's perspective. In this way, other regimes, including monarchies of the Lower Persian Gulf, that are NAM members, are unacceptable. An examination of Iranian Islamic, legal, and political values will help us better understand these positions.

Religious and Ideological Roots of the Policy

If one views the concept of non-alignment as being based on the idea of a balance, as do the advocates of the equidistance theory, one might note that the Koran makes several references to the term *equilibrium*. For instance, the Koran speaks of a divine natural equilibrium and advises people to avoid excess in their conduct and to maintain a balance between earth and heaven.[10] Allah, or God, has further contributed to this general notion of equilibrium, or the balance between the spiritual world and material world. This is accomplished by a juxtaposition between the symbol, iron, which represents power and the material world,[11] and the Koran, which symbolizes the spiritual by providing a source of the law and limits to political power.

Iranian non-alignment, however, is not based on equilibrium, in which one seeks harmony with one's environment.[12] The Koran states that God never leaves a path open for infidels to dominate the believers. This statement fuels the Muslim believers in their struggle against any form of foreign domination that would threaten their autonomy under divine sovereignty. In this regard, Iranian non-alignment is theoretically not in harmony with its environment. It is influenced by three Shia principles: Tawhid (Monotheism), Hakemiyat-e Illahi (Divine Sovereignty), and Jihad (Holy War).

Tawhid. Revolutionary Iran's non-alignment concept is rooted in monotheism, which is fundamental to understanding Islam.[13] Monotheism to Islam is so significant that the Koran refers to it in several places. Ali Shariati stated that Tawhid is not just one idea among others in Islam, but is the foundation of all Islamic principles.[14] Monotheism in Islam is clearly in opposition to the concepts of the Holy Trinity[15] in Christianity and Dualism[16] in Zoroastrianism. In this context, Islam does not sit on the fence and has no middle ground. In fact, from the start, the young Islamic state of Mohammed soon challenged both Christianity and Zoroastrianism, the state religions of the Roman and Persian Empires. These two regimes were the superpowers at the time Islam was emerging as a religion in the Arabian, Mesopotamian, and Mediterranean regions. The emerging Islamic state in Arabia did not align itself with either superpower, Persia or Rome, and neither did Revolutionary Iran.

Islamic monotheism refers to one God. According to the Koran, He is the sole ruler of the earth and heavens.[17] Moreover, He has neither a parent nor a child.[18] There is one community of believers (Umma)[19] and one path for salvation— Islam. According to Shariati's analysis of monotheism in Islam,[20] all other ideologies are only deviations from the true path. Islam remains the only true and legitimate path to God, who wishes real independence and security for people.[21] Thus, other religions are unacceptable for a true believer as a solution to worldly and spiritual problems. In the same way, Iranian non-aligned foreign relations strategy rejects the legitimacy of the Eastern and Western ideologies as man-made and materialistic in their approaches. Ayatollah Khomeini declared that both ideological camps operated in an unjust international system based on might and not right. He added that no state is truly independent unless it fights the dominant powers[22] and follows Islam.

Iran joined NAM mainly because the non-aligned states reject—at least in theory—superpower domination. Tehran, however, recognizes that not all NAM states practice what they espouse. Thus, Iranian non-alignment is not the same as that of other declared non-aligned states, upon which Ayatollah Khomeini casts a great deal of doubt.[23] In fact, the Ayatollah considered Iran to be a truly non-aligned state, which is rare.

Hakemiyat-e Illahi. The term *Islam* means submission to God, the only true Sovereign. According to the Koran, God is the Creator, the Sustainer, and Inheritor of all, as well as the Judge, the King, and the Sovereign. He is all powerful, owns the heritage of all heavens and the earth, and He ordains laws.[24] According to Shia theology, divine sovereignty passed from the Prophet Mohammed to the infallible imams and by extension to the most learned Faqih. In Revolutionary Iran, divine sovereignty is exercised by the Vilayat-e Faqih (rule of the leading jurisprudent) in the name of God and in the interest of Umma.[25] Thus, Iranian non-alignment takes a rather rigid stand on "sovereignty."

Some leaders argued that Iranian political chaos and injustice during the Qajars and Pahlavis were created by the loss of sovereignty to the Great Powers, particularly Britain and Russia. They cautioned against unchecked ties with the superpowers. This does not mean isolationism, as a few Iranian politicians have interpreted. On the contrary, most Islamic scholars do not advocate isolationism and have written a great deal about international law, treaties, and precedents that dictate the foreign relations, of one Muslim state with other Muslim and non-Muslim states. Islamic experts have spoken and written about the principle of peaceful co-existence, friendly relations with foreign states, alliances, trade relations and so on.[26] These principles protect one's sense of independence and identity while allowing interactions with other states.[27] In this regard, M. Mohammadi makes a similar argument based on Ayatollah Motahhari's views.

Jihad. Revolutionary Iran's non-alignment is also rooted in the concept of Jihad whose meaning is not limited to holy war. Focusing on Jihad only as a war has led some scholars to portray the Islamic world as rigid and prone to violent relations.[28] In fact, there are two types of Jihad—Jihad Asqar and Jihad Akbar. Jihad Asqar [the small holy war] occurs between an individual and his enemies without, while Jihad Akbar [the great holy war] occurs between an individual and the enemy within, or concupiscence.[29] Jihad is not solely a holy war. It also means confrontation, struggle, or challenge, which refers to its diplomatic as opposed to military connotation. Jihad's synonyms, especially struggle and challenge, refer to the symbolic value of Jihad. Like the term *war* in phrases such as "cold war" and "war against poverty," Jihad also has a symbolic utility. In Iran, the organization involved in improving the standard of living for the poor is called Jihad-e Sazandegi, or the Constructive Holy War.

Jihad, as a struggle of the powerless against the powerful, is a significant aspect of Iranian foreign policy. Iran's constitution requires the defense of the rights of Muslims everywhere.[30] According to Ayatollah Khomeini, there is an inevitable struggle between the Islamic Republic and the superpowers.[31] This struggle is not in the form of a full-fledged war, but rather as an ideological challenge.[32] In this struggle, the leadership insists there is not much difference between the East or West as to their goals or means, and there are fundamental differences between them and the Islamic state. In other words, Iran does not need to use violence when challenging the superpowers. This notion contradicts the view of those who believe that Islam was mainly spread by the sword. On the contrary, history shows that after Prophet Mohammed united the people of the Arabian Peninsula, he did not use military means against the Persians and Romans. Instead, he invited them to accept Islam.[33] In addition, Islamic historians put more emphasis on the Islamic ideological challenge than its military strength. They say that the miracle of Islam was to march victoriously into Mecca without violence and to spread it throughout Indonesia and among other Southeast Asian nations without its army. Nevertheless, Islam and its historical expansion have a rather negative connotation in the West.[34]

Legal/Constitutional Roots

The Constitution of the Islamic Republic of Iran makes several references to the concept of non-alignment.[35] While four constitutional articles address the general direction of foreign policy (Articles 152 through 155), one focuses particularly on non-alignment. According to Article 152, Iranian foreign policy is based on:

1. Protecting the independence and territorial integrity of the country.

2. Practicing non-alignment toward domineering states and mutual peaceful relations with non-domineering states.

3. Rejecting any form of hegemony.

4. Defending the rights of all Muslims.

Therefore, the constitution of this revolutionary regime associates three concepts with one another: the Islamic state, independence, and non-alignment. Based on the notion of the Islamic state, Article 56 declares that absolute sovereignty belongs to God, who has granted people the right to self-rule, which no ruler should deny. Thus, the constitution rejects the notion of dictatorship as well as foreign dominance. Moreover, it relates foreign dominance to dependence and attempts to end them both. A few examples regarding foreign advisors, treaties, and military bases will illustrate the point. First, although the need for industrialization is recognized by the constitution, which allows the hiring of consultants, Article 82 prohibits hiring foreign advisors unless it is absolutely necessary and then only with the approval of the Majlis (parliament). Second, any treaty that promotes foreign hegemony is void, according to Article 153. Finally, Article 146 explicitly prohibits the establishment of any foreign military bases in the country, even for peaceful purposes. This article is obviously in response to the prerevolutionary cases such as the British naval base in Bushehr, the Russian usage of the Anzali port facilities, and the American listening stations in northern Iran.

Political Base

From a political perspective, the non-alignment strategies of Revolutionary Iran and other states differ in regard to their attitudes toward the exiting global system, the nature of the policy, and the extent of cultural independence.

First, the founders of NAM accepted the concept of an ideologically divided world whose order was based on a balance-of-power system. From this perspective, their non-alignment strategy was a mechanical solution and a foreign policy option to cope with the status quo. The founder of the Islamic Republic, however, rejected this world order since it was perceived to be unjust and was forced upon the weaker nations.[36] He added that there was no significant difference between the behavior of the two superpowers because they were both materialistic, repressive in their own ways, and domineering toward the Third World. In his speeches, Khomeini put both superpowers in the same category: mustakberin (oppressors).[37] The Ayatollah added that Iran should continue its struggle with the superpowers in order to eliminate all dependencies.[38]

The second difference is that the founders of NAM did not intend to create a confrontational policy toward the superpowers. In fact, some NAM states even acted as a means of communication between the superpowers, as described in chapter 2. Iranian non-alignment is theoretically an active and quarrelsome policy that challenges the superpowers, although in practice Tehran has not consistently and constantly confronted the superpowers.

Finally, although all NAM states recognize the significance of cultural independence, explained in chapter 2, Ayatollah Khomeini went further in defense of cultural independence by insisting that the superpowers intended to destroy Islam. He stated that the problem of Iran had been "Gharbzadeqi,"[39] not industrialization, and that the two terms are not synonymous. J. Mansori also reached a similar conclusion, arguing that some developing countries mistakenly assume that the reason behind their national difficulties is their incompatibility with the West.[40] The Ayatollah added that the problem was the mental dependence of many educated people on non-Islamic values. As early as the Constitutional Revolution in 1905, the foreign-educated parliamentarians wrote the constitution and created the schools and courts based on foreign values.[41] For Khomeini, the most important aspect of independence was its cultural dimension, represented by Islam,[42] although some have argued that Revolutionary Iran has aimed equally at political, economic, and cultural independence.[43]

While Iranian leaders endorsed a non-aligned foreign policy, many also interpreted non-alignment differently, according to changing domestic and international circumstances. This led to three major trends in conducting foreign relations in the first decade of the revolution: a two-track policy (1979 to July 1982), a more conflictual policy (July 1982 to June 1985), and a more conciliatory policy (June 1985 to 1989).

A TWO-TRACK POLICY

This period lasted about two and one-half years. It began when Bazargan's government took charge in February of 1979 and ended when Iranian forces fought on Iraqi territory in July of 1982.[44] Moving the war led some observers to argue that Tehran was exporting its revolution. Although some Iranian leaders have insisted that exporting the revolution would be by word and not by sword,[45] there is evidence indicating that the nature of Iranian policy became less cooperative and more conflictual after Tehran gained the military initiative in the Iran–Iraq War.

The two-track foreign relations strategy consisted of one track oriented toward distancing Tehran from Washington and the other toward establishing more cooperative relations with Moscow. To distance itself from the United States, Iran took three major political measures, including withdrawal from CENTO, canceling the 1959 U.S.–Iran Defense Agreement, and declaring itself a non-aligned country. Considering that Iran under the Shah was one of the two closest allies of the United States in the region, Tehran's decision to shift from alignment with Washington to non-alignment was clearly viewed by American policymakers as a loss. Although Tehran also revoked Articles 5 and 6 of the 1921 Iran–U.S.S.R. treaty, from an American perspective Moscow achieved its goal of neutralizing Iran when Tehran joined NAM. The Soviet Union viewed the regional balance as moving more to its advantage when Iran severed ties with some Western allies (e.g., Israel), when it established closer relations with some Soviet allies (e.g., Syria), and when it canceled many Western military contracts. In general, foreign policy, and particularly non-alignment, during this period was considered by many Iranian leaders to be primarily a policy to reduce foreign, especially Western, influence in domestic affairs—a policy similar to Mossadegh's "Negative Equilibrium."[46] Since the Soviets did not have a significant presence in prerevolutionary Iran, they hoped to expand ties with the new regime.

Who was in charge of this interpretation of a non-aligned foreign policy? Although the new regime experienced several changes among the top governmental officials during this stage of the revolution, the actual source of power was Ayatollah Khomeini, who enjoyed the luxury of legitimizing their bids for leadership as they courted him for approval. In summarizing the nature and impact of leadership during this period, one may argue that Ayatollah Khomeini headed a coalition of secular and clergy leaders. Some experts suggested that moderate secular leaders were actually in control of foreign policymaking after the revolution.[47] The political base of this group, however, was so weak that it needed Ayatollah Khomeini's support to run the government. Thus, it was not an independent political force for policymaking, but the means for the clergy to conduct its policy. The power of the clergy soon became apparent when they began eliminating their rivals, starting with the moderates in November of 1979 and ending with members of the Tudeh party in 1982.[48]

In this period, Tehran began media campaigns against regional pro-Western states, although pro-Eastern ones were also not immune. Iran was soon blamed for a number of regional incidents of civil disobedience that varied from demonstrations and acts of sabotage to hijacking and even an attempted coup. Radical revolutionary idealists enjoyed freedom at the beginning of the revolution, such as establishing and operating centers like the Liberation Movement Office.[49] In light of this, it is conceivable that some of the regional acts of violence received somewhat more than just a blessing from the radical revolutionary idealists in Tehran, despite the denial of top government leaders. For instance, Hojatoleslam Rafsanjani has repeatedly denied Iranian intervention in such affairs.[50]

How genuine was Iranian non-alignment during this period? The behavior of revolutionary Iran initially seemed to be anti-Western and pro-Eastern. Thus, some concluded that Iranian non-aligned relations meant an American loss and a Soviet gain, but history showed that this conclusion was too simplistic and premature. To examine this topic closely, a discussion of Tehran's ties with Moscow and Washington is in order.

Relations with the Soviet Union

As mentioned earlier, Tehran's declaration of non-alignment at first meant that Moscow had achieved its post–World War II diplomatic goal of neutralizing Iran. It should be mentioned that the Soviets supported the NAM stance, especially for developing countries that they could not win as allies during the Cold War.[51] Thus, Moscow initially enjoyed a diplomatic advantage over Washington in dealing with Tehran, since Moscow was not viewed as a supporter of the Shah and had words of praise for Islam, the Iranian Revolution, and non-alignment.[52] Moreover, the Soviet Union had the advantage of maintaining its embassy in Tehran with ambassadorial representation. On the other hand, according to one expert, the United States had the diplomatic disadvantage of lacking an ambassador who could change the stereotype held by some influential religious–political figures.[53] More significantly, trade figures showed that Iranian trade with the Soviet Union and Eastern European states soared from 1979 to 1982, while Tehran's trade with the United States declined drastically.[54]

The Soviet advantages, however, did not lead to an alliance with Iran. In practice, Iran's non-alignment strategy used an equidistance approach by keeping Russia at bay while moving away from the United States. In practice, IMF trade statistics also illustrated that Iran maintained its strong economic ties with Western Europe and Japan despite the rise in trade with the Soviets and Eastern Europeans. For Tehran, non-alignment did not serve as a cover for a hidden alliance with Moscow. In fact, the Russians had a questionable image because of the negative connotation of Marxism in revolutionary Iran's sociopolitical values, the invasion of Afghanistan, their ties to the Tudeh party,[55] and the Soviet assistance to Iraq. As far as Iranian political values were concerned, Moscow resented being put into the category of a colonial power, since the Ayatollah referred to both superpowers as oppressors.[56] Top government officials also treated the superpowers similarly: on the same day they voided the 1959 Iran–U.S. Defense Agreement and Articles 5 and 6 of the 1921 Iran–U.S.S.R. treaty.[57]

The invasion of Afghanistan was a thorn in Tehran–Moscow relations. On 12 June 1979, the Ayatollah told the Soviet ambassador that "Soviet interference in [Afghanistan] would also have effects in Iran . . . and we ask the Soviet Union not to interfere in Afghanistan . . . when our youth say neither East nor West it means that neither [side] should interfere in Iran and the [position] is absolutely right."[58]

Nevertheless, this was the closest the two countries had been in the post–World War II period. The Soviets offered aid and weapons to Iran, although the latter did not enthusiastically receive the Soviet offers for weapons and technical assistance.[59] Also, the Russians halted arms deliveries to Iraq when the war broke out and applauded Tehran's anti-American rhetoric. During the 1979 Revolution, using its new strategic ties to Moscow, Tehran was able to deter American intervention. This experience of the new regime was different than Mossadegh's regime that was unable to thwart American intervention during the 1953 Coup. However, because of the Soviet invasion of Afghanistan, Iran joined the United States in boycotting the 1980 Olympics in Moscow.

Relations with the United States

Contrary to popular belief, the anti-American slogans of Iranian demonstrators did not signal an end to relations with the United States, although their actions should have served as a warning to allow a temporary cooling off period. Evidence indicates that the secular leaders of the revolution did not wish to cut off diplomatic ties with the United States. They knew that Tehran needed the West to balance the influence of the East and, on occasion, these leaders showed their positive intentions toward America. For instance, Foreign Minister Ibrahim Yazdi believed that relations with America would be possible if it stopped interfering in Iranian affairs. He stated that Iranians did not have any fonder memories of the Russians than they did of the Americans. Yazdi also referred to common ground between Tehran and Washington by emphasizing that "at least Americans believe in God."[60] Other secular leaders were willing to negotiate and to meet with U.S. officials. For example, Bazargan met National Security Adviser Zbigniew Brzezinski in Algiers in November of 1979.

In contrast, clerics were generally suspicious of American intentions and feared a 1953-style coup, especially after the United States admitted the Shah on 22 October 1979. For the clergy, the takeover of the American Embassy was an excellent opportunity to deter U.S. intervention by keeping Americans captive. In addition, it was a chance for the clergy to consolidate their power by eliminating secular leaders. Through the Algiers Agreement, the clergy ended the hostage crisis after it gained a pledge from America not to interfere in Iranian affairs. The fact that the crisis ended four months after the Iraqi invasion began also indicates that international concerns were secondary to Tehran.

On the second anniversary of the revolution, the clergy were pleased with their overall performance and confident that, unlike the Shah, they could lead the country without depending on America. On 20 April 1981, Ayatollah Khomeini stated that the Great Powers' propaganda was aimed at convincing the weaker nations that they were helpless and needed either the East or the West to run their countries, but Iran was the proof that their propaganda had been wrong.[61] Nevertheless, Tehran felt encircled by the East and the West: Iraq, equipped with Soviet and French arms, had invaded Iran; pro-Western Arab

Gulf states established the Gulf Cooperation Council; and the Soviets were in Afghanistan. When it seemed that the West was united against Iran, Ayatollah Khomeini began to emphasize self-reliance in his views on non-alignment.[62] Self-reliance was the main reason behind the significant growth in the Iranian domestic arms industry.[63]

Although Washington had a dual policy on Iran, the clergy suspected that America had instigated the Iraqi invasion. In May of 1982, Secretary Alexander Haig advocated a peaceful settlement that would "preserve the sovereignty and territorial integrity of both Iran and Iraq."[64] For Tehran, this gesture was too little and too late because Iran had begun to gain the strategic initiative in the war and was less willing to compromise. Meanwhile, Washington was leaning more toward Baghdad. This became apparent as the United States government removed Iraq from the list of terrorist states and granted it loans and credit.[65]

A MORE CONFLICTUAL POLICY

In the second phase of its non-alignment strategy (July of 1982 to June of 1985), Iran's foreign policy toward the superpowers was more conflictual and uncompromising, particularly regarding the settlement of the war. Iran's leaders referred to the war as the "imposed war" and believed that the superpowers were in full support of the Iraqi goal of destroying the Iranian Revolution.[66] Thus, Tehran's policy on the war serves as an indicator of its general non-alignment strategy, although the latter usually refers to a state's relations with the superpowers. Tehran's demand for the removal of President Saddam Hussein added to earlier suspicious about Iran's intervention in the domestic affairs of others and its attempts to export the Islamic Revolution. This rigid position put Iran under an international spotlight and isolated the country, which was also under a great deal of domestic pressure. Although Iran made some significant military achievements in the war (i.e., liberating most of its territory in 1982 and capturing the Manjoon Islands in 1984 and the Fao Peninsula in 1986), the nation had paid a high price in human and material losses.[67] To counter this pressure, Iran's leaders emphasized self-reliance and interpreted non-alignment as isolationism.[68]

Contrary to the earlier period, the clergy was in full control of all policymaking institutions after Khamene'i became president. The 1981 bombings, which killed many high-ranking revolutionary idealists (e.g., Beheshti, Raja'i, and Bahonar), had a major impact on Ayatollah Khomeini, who "withdrew his objection to the occupation of the highest offices of the state by clerics" and smoothed the way for the presidency of Ayatollah Khamene'i on 2 October 1981.[69] With the approval of Ayatollah Khomeini, the clergy put a rigid tone on the non-aligned nature of foreign relations. The reason for a more conflictual posture was a combination of some domestic and foreign successes, which led the leadership to become more adamant in pursuing its foreign policy goal toward the superpowers. Examples of domestic successes included winning ethnic support (e.g., the Arabs of Khozistan, Kurdish tribes, most Azeris, etc.), liberating lost territory, revitalizing the oil industry, and expanding the domestic arms industry. Regarding foreign policy successes, Iran moved the war into Iraqi territory, improved its trade relations, obtained supplies despite a ban on military sales, influenced the withdrawal of American forces from Lebanon after the Israelis' withdrawal, and succeeded in getting NAM to move its 1982 Summit from Baghdad to New Delhi.

Relations with the Soviet Union

Three issues negatively affected Tehran–Moscow relations: the dissolution of the Tudeh party, the existence of Soviet troops in Afghanistan, and Soviet support for Iraq. During 1982 and 1983, the coalition between the ruling clergy and the Tudeh Party ended when Tehran outlawed the Tudeh party and arrested its leading members. The crackdown followed the defection of a Soviet official who provided the Central Intelligence Agency with a list of Soviet agents in the Iranian government. In turn, the CIA passed the information on to Tehran.[70] The arrested party officers confessed to being agents of the Soviet Union during a highly publicized trial, which contributed to solidifying the position of the clergy. In fact, some argue that these confessions, obtained by force, provided the clergy with an excuse to publicly denounce the Tudeh party, although the Tudeh was not an immediate threat to the Islamic Republic.[71] Soon Tehran purged the military,[72] and Moscow severely criticized Tehran.[73] Iran then expelled eighteen Soviets in a diplomatic showdown.[74]

Although both Tehran and Moscow advocated an end to foreign intervention in Afghanistan, they were certainly on opposite sides of this issue. More than 100,000 Soviet troops remained in Afghanistan, while Iran assisted a select group of Mujahedin organizations[75] and housed more than 2 million Afghan refugees, without any aid from the United Nations.[76] Aiding the Afghan resistance at times led to some military skirmishes between Iranian forces and the Russians allied with their Communist Afghan forces.[77]

Close military ties between Moscow and Baghdad were another source of irritation in Tehran–Moscow relations. According to Ayatollah Khomeini, President Hussein was an atheist equipped with Soviet and Western arms.[78] In 1983, the Soviets alienated Iran even more by resuming arms shipments to Iraq. Soon Iran–Eastern bloc trade declined to its lowest level since the revolution.[79] In addition, natural gas negotiations between the two countries broke down.

Relations with the United States

Tehran–Washington relations hinged on three issues: the Israeli invasion of Lebanon, support of the Afghan Resistance, and the Iran–Iraq War. These issues had adverse effects on the relations between the two countries.

The Israeli invasion of Lebanon in June of 1982 contributed to a more conflictual relationship between Tehran and Washington. The invasion convinced some leaders that it was time to confront America. Ayatollah Khomeini resented the United States not only because it had supported the Shah, but because it traditionally supported Israel.[80] Soon after the Israeli invasion, Tehran sent a contingent of the Islamic Revolutionary Guard Corps (IRGC) to Lebanon. The IRGC began the indoctrination and training of Lebanese Shia Muslims in the Bekka Valley.[81] Thus, the Israeli invasion of Lebanon, like the Iraqi invasion of Iran, provided the Islamic Republic with the opportunity to export the revolution and challenge the regional status quo that favored the United States.

The bombings of the U.S. Embassy in Lebanon, the U.S. Marine barracks in Beirut, the U.S. Embassy in Kuwait, and the 1984 Kuwaiti hijacking should all be seen as part of this new confrontational policy of Revolutionary Iran toward America.[82] A direct link between Tehran and the four incidents is difficult to prove since the actions were carried out by the local Shia militia. One can, however, deduce that the actions must have pleased the idealists. Moreover, these incidents, which intended to minimize U.S. presence in Lebanon and elsewhere, paralleled the Iranian confrontational policy toward the superpowers. On 23 January 1984, the United States put Iran on the list of terrorist states and soon began to control its exports to Tehran.

Idealist leaders applauded the confrontational nature of Iran's foreign relations. Ayatollah Khomeini acknowledged its success by noting that the Lebanese Shia forced America to withdraw its marines from Lebanon (February 1984), although he did not mention who had inspired the Lebanese Shia and how. The tone and words of the idealists confirmed their confidence in the success of this strategy and their determination that they would not be intimidated by America. Idealists' confidence was apparent from their speeches and interviews. Dismissing allegations that Iran supported terrorism as an American presidential campaign ploy, Premier Mosavi argued, "We remind [President Reagan] of the events of Tabas [where the 1980 Desert One mission failed] and we warn that Reagan may face the same fate that befell Carter. "[83]

In Afghanistan, the United States and Iran were, in effect, strategic allies because they were pursuing similar foreign policy goals, including the withdrawal of the Soviets and the destabilization of the communist regime in Kabul. The revolutionary idealists, however, separated American and Iranian support for the Afghan Mujahedin by asserting that America wanted to promote a pro-American Islamic movement in Afghanistan.[84]

On the Iran–Iraq War, Tehran saw Washington and Baghdad as allies whose aim was to destroy the Islamic Republic. For Iran, the proof of such allegations was the support of Iraq by pro-American Arab Gulf states. Moreover, certain American actions convinced Iran that the United States was actively siding with Iraq, despite the U.S. declaration of neutrality in the war. Some of the pro-Iraqi American actions included providing military intelligence to Iraq, giving loans and credit to Baghdad, and reestablishing formal relations with Iraq in November of 1984. At the same time, Washington began Operation Staunch, refused to release frozen Iranian assets, and did not send to the Islamic Republic arms and parts for which the Shah's government had already paid. In 1992 revelations about the Bush administration's indiscriminate support of the regime of Saddam Hussein have shown that Iranian leaders were justified in this perception of the alliance between Washington and Baghdad against Iran before the Iraqi invasion of Kuwait.

For the revolutionary idealists, President Saddam Hussein's willingness to compromise[85] with Ayatollah Khomeini must have been a familiar scenario, reminiscent of the Shah's last days in power. This further encouraged the idealists to follow a conflictual policy. As international initiatives to bring about a cease-fire failed, Tehran became more isolated from other countries, especially the Great Powers.[86] Some also argue that Iran alienated others by its non-discriminatory, harsh, and rigid diplomatic posture. Interestingly enough, the alienation and isolation of Revolutionary Iran occurred despite its advantageous position to negotiate a settlement with Baghdad. Thus, Tehran's confrontational foreign relations position, which antagonized the major powers, seemed to line up the superpowers against it, as the extremist revolutionaries charged.

Generally, the non-aligned nature of Iranian foreign relations was genuine in this period. A Soviet scholar observed that the revolutionary clergy's struggle against "the Western devil" was balanced by a struggle against "the Eastern devil."[87] Tehran showed that its non-alignment posture did not favor either ideological camp by confronting equally the interests of both superpowers, which the Ayatollah called the "arrogant powers."[88] This policy was reminiscent of that of the seventh-century Islamic state that had simultaneously challenged the Roman and the Persian empires.

A MORE CONCILIATORY POLICY

The need for a more conciliatory approach in Iranian foreign relations was rooted in Tehran's failure to capture the strategic city of Basra, which has a significant Shia population. Despite inflicting heavy losses on the Iraqis, Iran lacked the hardware to break through the Iraqi defense.[89] Many revolutionary leaders realized that the conflictual approach to foreign policy limited Iran's ability to end the war on its own terms.[90]

From late 1984, the revolutionary realists began to emphasize that the non-aligned nature of foreign policy did not mean isolation from the rest of the world and aimed at changing the international image of Iran. On 28 October 1985, Khomeini confronted those idealists who had rejected relations with other governments. He decreed, "No man or wisdom accept [advocating isolationism] because its meaning is being defeated, annihilated, and buried."[91] Iranian foreign policy began showing conciliatory signs such as Tehran's efforts to resolve the TWA hijacking and end the radio propaganda war with the Soviets. Among other major signs of moderation were attempts to intervene on behalf of hostages in Lebanon. The latter, James Bill suggested, signaled the start of Iranian rapproachment.[92]

A survey of Iranian diplomatic behavior during this period shows that they emphasized dialogue more than defiance. From 1985, Iran–Eastern bloc ties began to expand. A year later, Iran's diplomatic relations with Western nations significantly improved despite the short-term downturn that occurred during the Salman Rushdie affair. The improvement of ties with the East and the West was an indicator of the revolutionary realists' growing influence in policymaking following signs of moderation by Ayatollah Khomeini. Furthermore, the Ayatollah's death and the emergence of Majlis Speaker Rafsanjani smoothed some of the rough edges in Iran's non-alignment strategy.

Relations with the Soviet Union

The improvement in Moscow-Tehran relations was due to a change in the perspective of Iran's leaders and a new Soviet approach by Mikhail Gorbachev. Soon the propaganda war softened and negotiations began.[93] By 1987, the Soviet media were already drawing a positive picture of the ties between the two states.

From 1986, Iran–Soviet trade and diplomatic activities showed major improvement. In February of 1989, Foreign Minister Eduard Shevardnadze visited Tehran. In June, Majlis Speaker Rafsanjani went to Moscow where the Russian and Iranian leaders signed a series of treaties, and Rafsanjani praised Gorbachev's domestic and international initiatives. Tehran–Moscow relations showed major improvement, which allowed Iran to play its Moscow card against Washington, particularly at the United Nations. For instance, after Foreign Minister Velayati's visit to Moscow in February of 1987, the Russians delayed the U.S.-proposed U.N. Security Council embargo on arms sales to Iran.[94] Nevertheless, relations were not immune from mishaps. In early 1988, Iranian demonstrators assaulted the Soviet Embassy, but both states soon began a process of damage control.[95]

By 1989, the three contentious issues in Iranian–Russian relations either became moot or lost their significance. The suppression of the Tudeh party was an issue that both sides refused to discuss; Soviet support for Iraq during the war also became a non-issue after Iran accepted U.N. Resolution 598 and Moscow insisted on assisting Tehran's reconstruction efforts to make up for their support for Baghdad;[96] and the Afghan crisis lost its urgency in the late 1980s as Soviet troops withdrew.

Considering the five non-alignment criteria stated earlier, these changes, however, did not mean a shift in Iranian foreign relations from a non-aligned to an aligned posture with the Soviet Union. Iran did not enter into any military pact with the Soviets, nor did it exclusively align itself with Moscow against

Washington. Additionally, the emerging revolutionary realists kept the growing cooperation with the Soviets in check by increasing their contacts with the West. Moreover, Iranian initiatives, particularly Majlis Speaker Rafsanjani's trip to Moscow, signified the start of Iran's reentry into the international community.[97]

In conclusion, Revolutionary Iran succeeded in resisting Moscow's pressures after 1979 despite its lesser military capability and lack of protection by the Western alliance. This success was caused in part by the opportunity that the breakdown of détente produced and in part by challenging the Soviets with an equally revolutionary ideology.

The Islamic component of a non-aligned foreign relations strategy provided Iran with an opportunity to put the Soviets on the defensive. In fact, Moscow became vulnerable to the agitation of Islamic populations in the Muslim-dominated republics when ethnic conflict intensified.[98] This did not lead to an ideological or military conflict between the two states, but it provided Tehran with more time and fewer foreign policy constraints. At the same time, the Soviets became occupied with their own domestic challenges and attempts to bring about a new order within and among the newly independent republics.

Relations with the United States

Since the emergence of the revolutionary realists was the main factor behind a more conciliatory policy toward the United States, one may ask whether the emergence of the realists was the result of external or internal pressures on Iranian society and government. The answer lies in a combination of the two. Although some experts consider the domestic factors to be more significant, others give more credit to external ones.

The roots of the revolutionary realists' bid to lead the foreign relations agenda date to public grievances that existed before the Majlis election in June of 1984. An increase in public criticism of the government led the Ayatollah to defend the Islamic regime in May 1984 and to respond with the comment, "Assuming that we [the clergy] are bad, but Islam is good . . . it is the Islamic duty to protect the Islamic Republic."[99] Also, there was a decline in public support for the war, and the number of military volunteers decreased. The response of the Ayatollah was to tell the IRGC commanders and the army, "Your faith must be strong despite your limited numbers."[100] These developments indicated public dissatisfaction with the policies and priorities of the Islamic government. A main target of criticism was the Iranian offensive strategy in Iraq which forced Ayatollah Khomeini to defend the Iranian military position by asserting that the revolutionary units were defending Islam and Iran and not attacking Iraq.[101] The public pressure finally led to the visible division among the leading revolutionary leaders into opposing camps.

These camps disagreed not only on certain domestic issues, but also on an appropriate approach to foreign relations, particularly on how to act toward the United States. For instance. Foreign Minister Velayati voiced a formal objection

This picture shows President Khamene'i of Iran during his address to the United Nations General Assembly on the anniversary of the Iraqi invasion of Iran. His trip to the U.S. to address the UN was considered a diplomatic signal that a more pragmatic group of revolutionary leaders were setting the tone of Iranian policy towards the end of the 1980s. *Photograph courtesy of UN/DPI Photo.*

to the September 1984 veto by the United States of the U.N. Security Council resolution on the withdrawal of Israeli forces from Lebanon. The more radical revolutionary idealists, however, went a step further in showing their opposition by applauding the bombing of the U.S. Embassy compound by the Lebanese.

Inviting West German Foreign Minister to Iran served as a trial for the more pragmatic and realistic leaders, who were awaiting a signal from Ayatollah Khomeini so they could begin to act. The signal came on 28 October when the Ayatollah declared that Iran must have relations with all countries and that severing relations with other governments was against the wisdom and law of Islam.[102] This was a major change in Iran's interpretation of its foreign relations based on non-alignment strategy. The need for a cooperative non-alignment strategy became even more apparent after Iraq and the United States formally reestablished diplomatic relations in November of 1984, but Iran made no concrete gesture toward the United States until mid–1985.

In order to change the international image of Iran, Majlis Speaker Rafsanjani initiated a tour of several countries in June of 1985 when, coincidentally, the hijacking of TWA Flight 847 took place. While in Syria, Rafsanjani met with Hezbollah members, and his efforts quickly and peacefully ended the incident.[103] Rafsanjani's success served to boost the emerging realists. In 1985 and 1986, Tehran facilitated the release of three American citizens held in Lebanon,[104] but this cooperative signal became a part of the Iran–Contra Affair.[105]

Both revolutionary realists and idealists had contributed to "Iran's America initiative."[106] According to the Tower Report, the Americans negotiated with the Iranians through two intermediaries—Manuchehr Ghorbanifar and Albert Hakim. The former was an Iranian businessman recommended by the Israelis and who had connections to Premier Musavi's office—a major center of the idealists. Albert Hakim was an Iranian-American businessman who became involved in the affair in January of 1986. He was reportedly linked to a relative of Majlis Speaker Rafsanjani. Ghorbanifar played a major role in the arms-for-hostage deal. The United States relied on him for five of the six arms transactions, despite the fact that he had failed a CIA-administered polygraph and that National Security Advisor Robert McFarlane did not trust him from the start.[107] This does not suggest, however, that the idealists had a change of heart about the "Great Satan." They only wanted American arms, the shortage of which had severely limited the ability of the Iranian military machine and became the main obstacle to a victory against Iraq. The goal of the idealists seemed clear from the intention and behavior of Ghorbanifar. According to Albert Hakim, Ghorbanifar intended to establish a system through which the United States would sell arms to Iran, Tehran would assist in releasing American hostages, and the Lebanese would take more hostages.[108] As far as his behavior was concerned, it appeared as though he was instructed to get American arms any way he could, even by exaggeration, misrepresentation, or fabrication.[109]

The reason for Ghorbanifar's resorting to questionable tactics lies in the difference between the approaches of the revolutionary idealists and realists to Iran's America initiative. The idealists must have viewed this initiative as a one-time deal with the "Great Satan." On the other hand, the realists' aim was to come to an informal, but cooperative, understanding with Washington. This was so despite the fact that they did not have a mandate from Ayatollah Khomeini for a more bold and all-encompassing change in the nature of Tehran–Washington relations.

Albert Hakim was the intermediary between the realists and U.S. officials. He was "the second channel" through which the Americans found out that Tehran did not have influence with all the Lebanese who held American hostages.[110] This information contradicted Ghorbanifar's exaggerated claims. The realists, however, did not meet with McFarlane in Tehran for two reasons. First, with no mandate from the Ayatollah, the realists were afraid of the wrath of the idealists.[111] Also, Ghorbanifar (not Hakim) had arranged the trip. During the congressional hearing, McFarlane indicated that the realist elements were concerned about the implications of a direct meeting with U.S. officials.[112]

On 3 November 1986, the Lebanese magazine *Al-Shira'* revealed the story of McFarlane's visit to Tehran, which hampered further contacts. The idealists' radical elements had leaked the news for two reasons: first, to keep Tehran and Washington apart by preventing further contact between the Americans and the realists;[113] and second, to retaliate against the realists who had arrested the leaders of the radical revolutionaries in October 1986.[114]

In reaction to the disclosure, the idealists pulled back, but Majlis Speaker Rafsanjani tried to salvage the process by giving positive signals to the United States until December of 1986.[115] The Reagan administration, however, was not receptive to these conciliatory gestures for the disclosure had created a major crisis.

In Iran, the idealists launched a campaign to blame the realists for the whole affair, and eight Majlis deputies demanded an investigation of the government's conduct that was similar to the American Iran–Contra hearings. The growing tension between the idealists and the realists prompted a call for unity from Ayatollah Khomeini. In addition, he blamed the whole affair on the "Great Satan" and declared its result a victory for Iran.[116] Actually, it was a victory for the realists who survived the idealists' campaign and succeeded in silencing the idealists' most radical faction.[117]

The year 1987 was a turning point in Tehran–Washington relations. Iran was becoming militarily weaker and diplomatically more conciliatory, while U.S. foreign policy was becoming more confrontational toward Iran. An analysis of this shift in American foreign policy is beyond the focus of this work, but it is sufficient to say that the change in policy was a result of several factors. These included the embarrassment following the Iran–Contra affair hearings, the success of the American air strike against Libya in April of 1986, the vulnerability of American forces in the Persian Gulf (as shown by the USS *Stark* incident in May of 1987), and the U.S. initiative to minimize the role of the Soviet Union in the Persian Gulf by reflagging Kuwaiti tankers.

The American lobby at the United Nations succeeded in obtaining the unanimous passing of Security Council Resolution 598 on 20 July 1987. It called for an immediate cease-fire in the Iran–Iraq War and the release of prisoners of war.[118] Iran did not reject the resolution, as the idealists demanded. Instead, it worked toward negotiating favorable preconditions before accepting it.

On the war with Iraq, a significant symbol of the realists' setting the policy agenda was their promise of a final offensive. This was in response to a decline in both public support for the regime and in Iran's military capability after a few large-scale operations. Iranian forces were losing their strategic initiative and had exhausted their supply sources. In January of 1987, the long-awaited Karbala 5 operation in southern Iraq did not break through the Iraqi defense although it caused very heavy losses. Also, Iran did not gain a symbolic breakthrough in May of 1987 when it launched the Karbala 10 operation in northern Iraq. By mid-1987, although it had gained the respect of the Pentagon for maintaining the military initiative against the well-equipped Iraqis, the Iranian military machine was losing its effectiveness.

On the American initiative to reflag Kuwaiti tankers, Iranian leaders were divided over an appropriate response. Proposals ranged from rhetoric to engaging U.S. forces. The idealists argued that the latter would raise the risk of American casualties and consequently lead to the withdrawal of the U.S. forces from the Persian Gulf, just as they had withdrawn from Lebanon in 1984. The realists, however, were more cautious in speculating on the consequences of a war with the United States, and the Persian Gulf was to become the testing ground.

In 1987 and 1988 the United States reacted guardedly to Iran's activities. It did not retaliate after the reflagged *Bridgeton* hit a mine in international waters during July of 1987. Washington, however, took bolder actions as it became evident that the Iranian military could not adequately respond. On 16 October 1987, an Iranian missile hit the U.S.-reflagged *Sea-Isle City*. Three days later, the United States retaliated by bombing an Iranian oil platform and boarding another to destroy its communication systems. On 26 October, Washington raised the stakes by imposing a total trade embargo on Tehran. The next episode of the Iran–U.S. military confrontation occurred in April of 1988, after the USS *Roberts* struck a mine. The United States retaliated by attacking a major Iranian oil platform. This time, Iranian forces opened fire on the U.S. Navy vessels which, in turn, sank three Iranian warships. The incident proved that Tehran was not capable of retaliating in any meaningful way despite Tehran's growing rhetoric. Confident about its military performance, the United States soon declared that it would protect all neutral shipping in the Persian Gulf. Also, Washington recognized that Tehran did not have a Moscow card to play at the time. Technically, Tehran might have had a Soviet card to play if it had played its hand correctly. However, Iran's Islamic approach to foreign policy created a number of differences over Afghanistan, Iraq, and the Arab–Israeli conflict that interfered with Moscow's taking more risks to prevent the projection of U.S. naval power into the Persian Gulf. Thus, the Islamic component of Iranian non-alignment strategy actually hurt Tehran's foreign policy by excluding the Soviet card from Iran's hand.

Despite harsh rhetoric, Tehran's responses to American retaliations soon became only diplomatic complaints and protests at the United Nations. Iran began to use international organizations as a place to score against Washington for it could not match U.S. firepower. Not only did Iran complain to the U.N. Security Council following the incident in April of 1988, but it also used the USS *Vincennes's* downing of an Iran Air passenger aircraft (which killed 290 Iranians and other nationals) in July of 1988 as an indicator of American aggression. Soon Tehran demanded an international investigation of the incident. Although Iran failed to win international condemnation of the United States in both the United Nations and the International Civil Aviation Organization (ICAO), the latter later faulted the United States for grave negligence.[119]

Ayatollah Khomeini's decision in July of 1988 to approve the U.N. cease-fire solidified the position of the realists, who soon accepted U.N. Resolution 598 without any preconditions. This event not only ended the direct influence of the idealists on the foreign policy agenda, but it also closed the chapter on Iran–U.S. military clashes. After Resolution 598 took effect on 20 August 1988, the United States reduced its naval presence in the Persian Gulf. The reduction led the realists to claim a victory because Iranian leaders had been concerned that American forces might remain in the area to destabilize the revolutionary regime.

Although the diplomatic environment was encouraging in August of 1988, the Republican administration shied away from engaging in a dialogue with Iran, which could have interfered with Vice-President George Bush's bid for the presidency. Conversely, the diplomatic scene was active in Tehran, where the realists were on the rise, while the idealists were losing leverage over policymaking. For instance, *Le Monde* reported that Premier Mosavi's main reason for resigning was his lack of influence on Iranian foreign policy.[120]

The publication of Rushdie's *The Satanic Verses* in early 1989 provided the revolutionary idealists with an opportunity to shake up Iranian foreign policy. This event had the potential of changing the direction of foreign relations in general. Ayatollah Khomeini, supported by the idealists, not only declared *The Satanic Verses* to be a blasphemy, as other clerics throughout the Islamic world had done earlier, but also issued a death sentence on Salman Rushdie.[121] Western reaction to this sentence energized the idealist forces and put the realists on the defensive. Prime Minister Musavi was the first government official who spoke on this issue after the Ayatollah declared February 14 to be a day of mourning for the publication of the book.[122] But President Khamene'i suggested that Rushdie might be pardoned if he apologized to Muslims and Ayatollah Khomeini and warned Iranians against storming the British Embassy.[123] The Ayatollah rejected Rushdie's statement of regret and renewed the call for his death.[124] This action forced President Khamene'i to retract his earlier comments about pardoning Rushdie.[125]

The timing of the idealists in the Rushdie affair was no coincidence as it occurred when the diplomatic atmosphere between Iran and the West, particularly the United States was warming up. The realists were orienting Iranian revolutionary energy toward domestic issues and had outlined a reconstruction policy.[126] They were also sending cooperative signals on foreign policy issues. In November, Majlis Speaker Rafsanjani commented that Iran should drop its crude diplomacy in order to avoid making enemies.[127] He offered to assist the United States with the hostages in Lebanon if America released Iranian assets.[128] In January of 1989, President Bush implied in his inaugural speech that cooperation would be rewarded. Soon President Khamene'i stated that better relations with Washington could be possible if the United States released frozen Iranian funds and weapons.[129] Meanwhile, Minister Velayati toured two European NATO capitals to signal Tehran's cooperative diplomatic posture. In fact, he arrived unexpectedly in London for talks with Minister Geoffrey Howe.[130] Then during a visit to Spain, he signed a memorandum of understanding with his Spanish counterpart that called for expansion of economic, industrial, and trade ties.[131] A day before Ayatollah Khomeini's decree, Minister Velayati was in Muscat to expand bilateral relations with another pro-American regime.[132]

Contrary to the idealists' expectation, the Rushdie affair turned out to be a short-lived crisis.[133] There were two reasons. First, the conditions of this affair were different from the 1979 hostage crisis. Second, it seemed as though the West (especially the United States) had learned to ignore the revolutionary rhetoric. The Rushdie affair was "the last hurrah of the radicals" in the first decade of the revolution. While its impact only temporarily halted the realists' campaign to improve Iran's image, many realists adopted a hard-line posture on some foreign policy issues to protect their position and redeem their revolutionary credentials. For example, Rafsanjani called on the Palestinians to attack Americans and other Westerners in retaliation for Palestinians killed by Israel,[134] although he later retracted the statements by arguing that they had been distorted.[135] The realists eventually maintained their power as the idealists lost their source of inspiration when the Ayatollah died.[136] Three domestic events also solidified the position of the realists: Khamene'i's succession of Khomeini, Rafsanjani's successful bid for the presidency, and the amending of the Iranian constitution in 1989.

As the realists secured their positions, Tehran began to show more positive signs toward the United States. On 8 June, Rafsanjani again offered to assist with the release of American hostages if the United States helped with Iranian hostages in Lebanon.[137] On 2 July, Finance Minister Irvani stated that Tehran would seek out Western technology when it was superior to Soviet technology.[138] On 22 August when Rafsanjani outlined his foreign policy, "neither East nor West" was cited as the policy directive[139] despite the calls by former Minister Mohtashemi, a well-known revolutionary idealist, for a new anti-American policy.[140] In October, during his first presidential news conference, Rafsanjani repeated his offer to assist America in locating and releasing Western hostages in Tehran.[141]

Since mid–1989, Iran's political approach toward the United States has been so positive that on the tenth anniversary of the storming of the U.S. Embassy, only a small number of demonstrators turned out to listen to former Minister Mohtashemi, who was the main speaker at the ceremony.[142] Two days later, the United States agreed to free $567 million in frozen Iranian assets.[143] Moreover, the U.S. State Department's legal adviser held unannounced talks with Iranian officials to inform them that the U.S. wanted to compensate the families of the passengers killed in the July 1988 airbus incident.[144] Other positive gestures by Tehran and Washington included Iran's decision to allow a U.N. inspector to investigate human rights practices and abuses[145] and the decision by the United States to withhold from publishing a report on Iranian involvement in state terrorism.[146] By February of the next year, the realists felt so secure that President Rafsanjani commented that Ayatollah Khomeini's call for Salman Rushdie's death was the view of one expert and was therefore susceptible to debate.[147]

In sum, Iranian non-alignment strategy toward the United States generally became more cooperative beginning in 1985. Contrary to the earlier uncomplimentary comments about America and its hegemonic influence at the United Nations,[148] President Khamene'i visited New York in 1987 to address the U.N. General Assembly on the anniversary of the Iraqi invasion. Iran also began to use international organizations, some of which it lobbied for condemnation of the United States after the airbus incident in 1988.[149] This in itself indicated a softening in the nature of Iran's policy, whose goal in the confrontational period would have been to settle the score with the United States by engaging American or pro-American forces in the region instead of using diplomatic means to settle the issue.

NOTES

1. For information about its historical background, structure, and function, see Zia H. Hashmi, *Iran, Pakistan, and Turkey: Regional Integration and Economic Development* (Lahore Pakistan: Aziz Publishers, 1979), 73-122.

2. For instance, see S. T. Hunter, *Iran and the World: Continuity in a Revolutionary Decade,* (Bloomington: Indiana University Press, 1990).

3. Robert Graham, *Iran: The Illusion of Power* (New York: St. Martin's Press, 1980), 245-54.

4. For instance, see Rohollah Khomeini, *Sahife-i Nur*, vol. 18 (Tehran: Sazman, Madarik, Farhangi, Inqilab, Islami Vabastah Bih Vizarat Farhang va Irshad Islami, 1986), p. 91.

5. See IMF, *Directions of Trade Statistics* (Washington: World Book Publication, 1964, 1968, 1972, 1976).

6. *Payam-e Emrooz*, 9 May 1979.

7. *Jomhori-e Islami*, 5 March 1983.

8. *Kayhan Havai*, 2 May 1990.

9. Foreign Broadcasting Information Service, *Daily Report: Near East & South Asia* (henceforth FBIS/NE-SA), 10 December 1979.

10. *Koran*, Sura Al-Rahman, nos. 7-9.

11. *Koran*, Sura Al-Hadid, no. 25.

12. *Koran*, Sura Al-Nesa, no. 141.

13. *Koran*, Sura Al-Baqara, no. 163; Sura Al-Nahl, no. 22; Sura Al-Moa'- menon, nos. 91-92; Sura Al-Safat, no 4; Sura S, no. 65; Sura Al-Ekhlas, no. 1.

14. See Ali Shariati, *Islamshenasi* [Understanding Islam], (Mashhad, Iran: Chapkhaneh-i Tus, 1968), 73.

15. *Koran*, Sura Al-Maa'da, nos. 75-76.

16. *Koran*, Sura Al-Nahl, no. 51.

17. *Koran*, Sura Al-Forgan, os. 61-62; Sura Al- Oa'mran, no. 180; Sura Al-Safat, nos. 4-5.

18. *Koran*, Sura Al-Ekhlas, no. 3.

19. *Koran*, Sura Al-Hajarat, no. 13.

20. See Shariati, 70-129.

21. Author's interview with Professor Abdulaziz Sachedina, Department of Religious Studies, University of Virginia (Charlottesville, Virginia: fall 1989).

22. R. K. Ramazani, ed., *Iran: Challenge and Response in the Middle East*, rev. (Baltimore, Md.: Johns Hopkins University Press, 1988), 27-29.

23. Ibid, 22.

24. *Koran*, Sura Al-Baqara, nos. 29 & 117: Sura Al-An'am, no. 73, Sura Al'A'raf, no. 54; Sura Hud, nos. 6-7; Sura Al-Ra'd, nos. 16-17; Sura Al-Anbiya', nos. 30-33; Sura Al-O'mran, no. 180; Sura Al-Hajar, no. 23; Sura Maryam, no. 40; Sura Al-Nesa, no. 40; Sura Al-Nas, no. 2; Sura Al-Loqman, no. 9 and Sura Al-Zumar, no. 1; Sura Al-O'mram, no. 180, Sura Al-Hajar, no. 23; Sura Maryam, no. 40; and Sura Al-A'la, no.3.

25. For more information, see Abdulaziz Sachedina, *Islamic Messianism: The Idea of Mahdiin Twelve Shiaism* (Albany: State University of New York Press, 1981).

26. See Siyd Khalil Khalilian, *Hoqoq-e Biy Al-Milal-e Islami* [Islamic International Law], vol. 1 (Tehran: Office of Publications of'Islamic Culture, 1362 [1983]), 203-76.

27. M. Mohammadi, *Osol-e Siyasasat-e Khareji-e Jomhori-e Islami-e Iran*, [The Principles of the Foreign Policy of the Islamic Republic of Iran] (Tehran: Amir Kabir, 1987), 47-49.

28. Majid Khadduri, *War & Peace in the Law of Islam* (Baltimore, Md.: Johns Hopkins University Press, 1955).

29. A'skar Hoqoqi, *Falsafe-i Siyasi-i Islam* [Political Philosophy of Islam], vol. 1 (Tehran: Arin, 1975), 60-62.

30. See *The Constitution of the Islamic Republic of Iran*, Article 152.

31. Ramazani, 21.

32. Ibid., 19-54.

33. For reference to the role of invitation and missionary activities, see Abolfazi Shakori, *Feqh-e Siyasi-e Islam* [Religious Politics of Islam], vol. 2, (Tehran: Arin, 1982), 356-81.

34. For an analysis of negative perceptions of Islam, see Maxime Rodinson, *Europe and the Mystique of Islam*, trans. by Roger Veinus (Seattle: University of Washington Press, 1987).

35. For example, see Articles 3, 82, and 146.

36. Ramazani, 21.

37. See *Sahife-i Nur*, vol. 11, p. 17.

38. Ibid., 266.

39. This term literally means "Westoxication" but it generally means adopting foreign values that include both the East or the West as the source of inspiration. However, the Ayatollah was not the first to refer to Iranian cultural dependence. See Jalal Al-Ahmad, *Gharbzadeqi* [Westoxication], reprint (Solon, Ohio: Union of Societies of Islamic Students, 1979).

40. J. Mansori, *Farhang-e Isteglal* [The Culture of Independence] (Tehran: Ministry of Foreign Affairs, 1987), 1-4.

41. *Sahife-i Nur*, vol. 11, pp. 183-94.

42. *Sahife-i Nur*, vol. 12, p. 122.

43. Mansori, 251.

44. It should be noted that some experts point to significant events in the first two to three years of the Iranian Revolution, including the takeover of the U.S. Embassy (November 1979) and the fall of President Abolhassan Bani-Sadr (June 1981), and divide this two and a half year period into shorter time spans in order to analyze Iranian foreign policy moves in more detail. Although there is a great deal that one can learn from more detailed actions of revolutionary Iran, this study focuses on a larger scope while at the same time it does not lose sight of minor events that contributed to shifts in policy. Thus, while an analysis of Iran's foreign policy during the different administrations of Bazargan, Bani-Sadr, Raja'i, or Khamene'i is not included in this particular study, it would make an interesting topic for further research.

45. Ayatollah Khomeini's 9 August 1980 speech in *Sahife-i Nur*, vol. 12 (Tehran: Ministry of Islamic Guidance, January-February 1983), 283. Also see Hojatoleslam Khamene'i's speech on 28 March 1980 in *Dar Maktab-e Jom'eh*, vol. 2 (Tehran: Ministry of Islamic Guidance, January 1986), 87.

46. S. Zabih, *The Mossadegh Era* (Chicago: Lakeview Press, 1982), 88-96.

47. M. Behrooz, "Trends in the Foreign Policy of the Islamic Republic of Iran, 1979–1988," in *Neither East Nor West*, ed. Nikki R. Keddie (New Haven, Conn.: Yale University Press, 1990).

48. For a detailed analysis of the domestic political struggle, see S. Bakhash, *The Reign of the Ayatollahs*, rev. ed. (New York: Basic Books, 1986).

49. Helen Metz, *Iran: A Country Study* (Washington D.C.: U.S. Government Printing Office, 1989), 222-24.

50. See his 18 December 1981 speech in *Dar Maktab-e Jome'h*, vol. 4 (Tehran: Ministry of Islamic Guidance, Summer 1988), 152.

51. For the Soviets' emphasis on non-alignment policy in the Third World, see R. Allison *The Soviet Union and the Strategy of Non-Alignment in the Third World* (Cambridge: Cambridge University Press, 1988).

52. Leonid Medvedko, "Islam and the Liberation Revolution," *New Times,* 43 (October 1979): 18-21.

53. See R. W. Cottam, *Iran and the United States*, (Pittsburgh: University of Pittsburgh Press, 1988), 209.

54. IMF, *Direction of Trade Statistics* (Washington: World Book Publication, 1982, 1986, 1990).

55. "Red Plot Sparks Off Anti-Russian Frenzy," *London Sunday Times*, 8 May 1983, p. 18.

56. *Sahife-i Nur*, vol. 11, p. 17.

57. R. K. Ramazani, "Iran's Foreign Policy: Contending Orientation," in *Iran's Revolution: The Search for Consensus*, ed. R. K. Ramazani (Bloomington: Indiana University Press, 1990), 51-52.

58. *Sahife-i Nur*, vol. 7, p. 89.

59. See Hunter, 95-96.

60. See Gary Sick, *All Fall Down: America's Tragic Encounter with Iran*, (New York: Penguin Books, 1986), 168-69.

61. *Sahife-i Nur*, vol. 14, pp. 193-95.

62. *Sahife-i Nur*, vol. 14, p. 194.

63. *MEED* 30, no. 29 (19 July 1986): 4-6. *MEED* 31, no.8 (2 May 1987): 11. *Jane's Defense Weekly*, 23 July 1988, pp. 126-31.

64. See the address by Secretary Alexander Haig on 26 May 1982 before the Chicago Council on Foreign Relations (transcript in *American-Arab Affairs* 1, (Summer 1982): 190-96).

65. See Nader Entessar "Superpowers and Persian Gulf Security: The Iranian Perspective," *Third World Quarterly* 10, no. 4 (October 1988) 1437.

66. *Sahife-i Nur*, vol. 14, pp. 107-108.

67. Metz, 271-78.

68. *Sahife-i Nur*, vol. 17, pp. 151-55.

69. Said Amir Arjomand, *The Turban for The Crown: The Islamic Revolution in Iran* (New York: Oxford University Press, 1985),154.

70. *New York Times*, 20 November 1986.

71. See R. Hermann, "The Role of Iran in Soviet Perceptions and Policy," in Kiddie, ed., 77-78.

72. "Iran Executes 10 Communists," *Washington Post*, 26 February 1984.

73. V. Komarov, "Reign of Terror Against Patriots," *New Times* 21 (May 1983):. 10-11.

74. Other experts also point out that Iran, and not the Soviet Union, initiated this diplomatic confrontation (see Hunter, 87).

75. "Afghan Rebels Describe Training in Iran," *FBIS/International Affairs*, 1 June 1988, p. 11; "Afghan Resistance Groups," *Defense Journal* 12, no. 12 (1987), 43-44.

76. "Iran: Sanctuary for Millions," *MEED* 30, no. 4 (25 January 1985): 5.

77. Hunter, 86.

78. *Sahife-i Nur*, vol. 14, p. 155.

79. IMF, *Directions of Trade Statistics*.

80. Hunter, 59.

81. R. K. Ramazani, *Revolutionary Iran*, 184.

82. See Robin Wright, *Sacred Rage*, rev. ed., (New York: Simon and Schuster, 1986).

83. "Prime Minister Views Elections, US Bullying," *FBIS/SA*, 19 April 1984, p. I-1.

84. On the concept "pro-American Islam," see *Sahife-i Nur*, vol. 18, pp. 36-37. On the role of the United States in Afghanistan, see the same source, pp. 116-17.

85. In May 1982, Iraq was forced to withdraw from east of the Shatt Al-Arab after an Iranian counteroffensive. In April of 1984, President Hussein proposed a meeting with the Ayatollah (Metz, 274-75).

86. See A.H.H. Abidi, "Iran and Non-Alignment," *International Studies* 20, nos. 1-2 (January-June 1981): 357.

87. A. Y. Yodfat, *The Soviet Union and Revolutionary Iran* (New York: St. Martin's Press, 1984), 94.

88. For example, see *Sahife-i Nur* vol. 14, p. 194.

89. For details of this operation, see Metz, 276.

90. "Iranian Minister Defends Policy," *Washington Post*, 27 November 1986.

91. *Sahife-i Nur*, vol. 19 (January-February 1983): 73.

92. See James Bill, "The New Iran: Relations with Its Neighbors and the United States," *Asian Update* (August 1991).

93. "Iran–Soviet Cooperation to Start," *Keyhan* (21 February 1985): 2.

94. *FBIS USSR/International Affairs* (19 February 1987): 13-14.

95. Ibid., 27.

96. "Moscow Wants Role in Reconstruction," *MEED* 32, no. 47 (9 November 1988): 19.

97. R. K. Ramazani "Iran's Resistance to the U.S. Intervention in the Persian Gulf" in Kiddie, ed., 57.

98. On the Soviets' concerns about the impact of revolutionary Islam on their Muslim republics, see "Mullahs, Mujahedin, and the Soviet Muslims," *Problems of Communism* (November/December 1984): 28-44.

99. *Sahife-i Nur,* vol. 18, p. 285.

100. *Sahife-i Nur,* vol. 18, p. 284.

101. *Sahife-i Nur,* vol. 18, pp. 20-21 and vol. 17, pp. 230-31.

102. *Sahife-i Nur,* vol. 19, pp. 72-74.

103. Wright, 277.

104. Benjamin Weir was released on 15 September 1985, Lawrence Jenco on 26 July 1986, David Jacobson on 2 November 1986; see *Congressional Quarterly's Editorial Research Reports* 2, no. 8 (26 August 1988): 435-38.

105. For a comprehensive report of this affair, see *The Tower Commission Report: The Full Text* (New York: Bantom Books and Times Books, 1987).

106. R. K. Ramazani, *Revolutionary Iran*, 253.

107. *Tower Report,* 40

108. R. K. Ramazani, *Revolutionary Iran*, 258.

109. Ibid.

110. Ibid., 262.

111. Ibid., 257.

112. *Tower Commission*, 298.

113. Although the initial meetings between the American and Iranian officials were arranged by the intermediaries of the idealists, Washington succeeded in meeting representatives of the realists in later meetings. The first meeting took place between Oliver North and a representative of the prime minister's office in February of 1986 (*Tower Report,* 249-50). The second meeting occurred in Tehran during McFarlane's trip to Tehran. The third meeting was during a CIA-arranged trip of a relative of Rafsanjani to Washington in September of 1986. The last meeting, which took place in Frankfurt, was arranged by Albert Hakim in October of 1986 (Ramazani, *Revolutionary Iran*, 258-59).

114. Ramazani, *Revolutionary Iran*, 263-64.

115. *FBIS/SA*, 5 December 1986.

116. *FBIS/SA*, 20 November 1986.

117. Metz, 223-24.

118. For the text of the resolution, see *New York Times*, 21 July 1987, p. A1.

119. See "World Aviation Panel Faults US Navy on Downing of Iran Air Jet," *New York Times*, 4 December 4, 1988, p. 3.

120. *FBIS*, 13 October 1988.

121. *New York Times,* 15 February 1989, p. A1.

122. *FBIS*, 14 February 1989.

123. *New York Times*, 18 February 1989, p. A1.

124. *Washington Post*, 20 February 1989, p. A1.

125. *Washington Post*, 23 February 1989, p. A1.

126. *FBIS*, 20 October 1988. Focusing on domestic issues, the Majlis approved the first five-year plan of the government starting in March of 1989 (*FBIS*, 17 October 1988). Majlis Speaker Rafsanjani initiated a merger of the IRGC (a center for younger radicals) with the Army (*FBIS*, 20 October 1988).

127. *FBIS*, 21 November 1988.

128. *Washington Post*, 26 November 1988, p. A1.

129. *New York Times*, 6 February 1989, p. A1.

130. *Washington Post*, 8 February 1989, p. A35.

131. *FBIS*, 10 February 1989.

132. *FBIS*, 13 February 1989.

133. At its height, the crisis lasted from 20 February, when the European Economic Community members decided to recall their top diplomats from Tehran (*New York Times*, 21 February 1989), to 20 March, when EEC foreign ministers agreed that their diplomats could return to Tehran (*Washington Post*, 21 March 1989).

134. *FBIS*, 5 May 1989 and *Washington Post*, 6 May 1989.

135. *Washington Post*, 11 May 1989, p. A1; *New York Times,* 11 May 1989, p. A3.

136. *Washington Post*, 4 June 1989, p. A1.

137. *FBIS*, 8 June 1989.

138. *Washington Post*, 3 July 1989, p. A1.

139. *FBIS,* 23 August 1989.

140. *New York Times*, 8 August 1989, p. A6.

141. *Washington Post*, 24 October 1989, p. A27; *New York Times*, 24 October 1989, p. A10.

142. *Washington Post*, 5 November 1989, p. A42. Also see *FBIS*, 6 November 1989.

143. *Washington Post,* 7 November 1989, p. A14; *Washington Post*, 13 November 1989, p. A1.

144. *New York Times*, 8 November 1989, p. A14.

145. *New York Times*, 3 December 1989, p. 8.

146. *Washington Post*, 16 December 1989, p. A22.

147. *Financial Times*, 19 February 1990.

148. For instance, see *Sahife-i Nur*, vol. 17, pp. 190.

149. Iran complained to the International Court of Justice. The U.S. and Iran eventually agreed to a $131.8 million settlement for the July 1988 downing of Iran Air Flight 655 by the USS Vincennes in the Strait of Hormuz. See *Washington Post*, 2 February 1996.

6

CONCLUSION

There is no standard for typical behavior of revolutionary states. The previous chapters indicate that there are clear differences in behavior between China, Cuba, and Iran; yet, there are also significant similarities in their patterns of foreign relations as we shall see.

DIFFERENCES IN FOREIGN POLICY STRATEGIES

The differences among the Chinese, Cuban, and Iranian strategies were primarily the result of their diverse backgrounds and the different sets of regional conditions with which they had to cope. The major differences included factors such as size and national wealth, military capabilities, leadership, institutional means, and the nature of their foreign policies.

Size and National Wealth

Since the size and national wealth of any state contributes considerably to the formulation and implementation of its foreign policy, it is essential to note that the three states were significantly diverse in these respects. In terms of size, Iran ranked between Cuba and China. Its per capita gross national product (GNP) was the highest of the three. Iranian national income, however, had one main source of revenue—oil. Despite Iran's wealth, the quality of life for an average Iranian did not match that of an average Cuban or Chinese.[1] Although China's per capita GNP was far less than that of Cuba or Iran,[2] it surpassed both in size and national wealth. In fact, the People's Republic of China not only had an impressive population and area, but its natural and human resources were unmatched by the other two. Cuba was the smallest of the three in both population and resources.[3] There was, however, less economic inequality among the Cubans who also enjoyed a higher standard of living, especially in terms of education and health care among most developing nations.

Thus, there were significant differences among the states in size and wealth which, consequently, gave different weights in a global context to their statuses as revolutionary states. In this respect, China was more willing to act as an independent entity in comparison to Cuba and Iran. Havana was less able to resist domestic and international economic pressures and thus became more economically dependent on Moscow. Finally, the economic power of Iran had, for the most part, been conditioned by the level of international demand for petroleum and the price of crude oil.

Military Capability

Considering that foreign policy is often more effective with appropriate military strength, a revolutionary regime is influenced not only by its size and wealth but also by military capability. In this respect, the capability of the three states varied. Generally speaking, China easily outclassed Iran and Cuba even before it joined the nuclear club or developed sophisticated missile technology.[4] The PLA became an effective force because of its experiences during the Chinese civil war, the Japanese invasion, and the Korean War. This quality led Beijing to act more independently from both superpowers in comparison to the other two states.

Despite Cuba's size, its military machine proved to be effective during the Bay of Pigs invasion, the Ethiopia-Somalia War, and the Angolan Civil War. Cuba's military capability did not match China's but surpassed Iran's. Within the Caribbean basin, Cuba had the most effective and experienced military machine. In fact, Cuba's military victories gave a more militant context to the foreign policy of this small island nation.

As a result of its close military ties to the United States in the prerevolutionary days, Iran possessed some of the most sophisticated military equipment compared to the other two states. Its combat military performance, though, was a different matter. While Tehran's military machine had once been a force with which to be reckoned in the region, its capability decreased significantly after the revolution.[5] In fact, Iranian military strength declined so drastically that it became vulnerable to most of the regional powers like Turkey, Pakistan, and particularly Iraq. I must add that while Ankara and Islamabad did not capitalize on Iran's vulnerability, Baghdad did. Consequently, Tehran could effectively project its military might only toward the smaller Arab states of the Persian Gulf.[6] In contrast, because they were not as dependent as Tehran on foreign technology, the military capabilities of Havana and Beijing did not decline as significantly after their revolutions.

Leadership

Considering that leadership directly influences the nature and direction of public policy in most states, especially those in the developing world, it is essential to compare the revolutionary leaders of these states. One should recognize that the foreign relations of the three regimes were directed by different types of leaders.

Mao and most of those leading the 1949 Revolution in China were former peasants committed to Marxism and supported at least nominally by Moscow.[7] From the beginning, however, relations between the communist Chinese and the Soviet leaders were problematic at best. Not expecting the ascendancy of the CCP's leaders to power, the Soviets had extensive ties with the Chinese nationalist leaders who had provided the Soviets with many special privileges. For the Chinese communist leaders, the relevance of the suggestions and solutions of the Soviet Union Communist Party (SUCP) for China were questioned even before the communists came to power.[8] Moreover, the CCP leaders believed in the egalitarian notion of Marxism and would not take a second seat to the SUCP leaders.

In contrast to most of the Chinese and Iranian leaders, Castro came from both an upper class family and was a college educated lawyer by profession.[9] While the CCP leaders showed signs of a pro-Soviet stance in the days before the Chinese Revolution, Castro did not. In fact, throughout the years of struggle against the dictator Batista Y Zaldivar, the leaders of the 26 July movement and the SUCP kept their distance. Moreover, the Soviets supported Cuba's Urban Socialist party while Castro's band was mostly supported by the Cuban peasants. Additionally, Castro and his associates had not earned the trust of the Soviets who, until Castro declared that the Cuban Revolution was a socialist one, thought of them as part of the liberal bourgeoisie.

Iranian leaders were very different from their counterparts in Cuba and China. They were mostly middle class Shia Muslim clerics with a distaste for European ideologies, especially Marxism with its atheistic message. Moreover, the revolutionary clergy were not from the upper ranks of the Shia hierarchy. Before Ayatollah Montazeri was chosen as the successor, Ayatollah Khomeini was the only high ranking cleric among the top leaders, and even he was not initially one of the few "Grand Ayatollahs." Furthermore, while the Chinese and Cubans had an affinity for the Soviets in their struggles against the Americans, the clergy disliked both superpowers.

Institutions

The institutional means of their non-alignment strategies were also different among the three states. By the time of the revolution, the Chinese had a more elaborate organizational structure than either the Cubans or the Iranians. Established in 1921, the CCP survived the 1927 and 1934–1935 KMT campaigns, the Japanese invasion, and the Long March. Thus, the turbulent history of the CCP provided many Chinese party leaders with both the military experience they needed to survive and the organizational skills necessary to govern. Within the CCP structure, Mao had a good deal of power but there were also other powerful individuals advocating a decentralized distribution of power. In fact, despite his mass appeal, Mao was occasionally left out of the party politics such as during the Eighth Party Conference in 1956. One major impact of this decentralization of power was that the issue of membership in NAM was left out of the Chinese political agenda. In contrast, the institutional positions of Castro and Khomeini were more secure.

In comparison to China, Castro's close-knit group was a very small operation. Generally speaking, the Fidelistas advocated the notion that a small, ideologically committed and professionally experienced group would be sufficient to defeat a powerful enemy. In contrast, Mao repeated that "political power grows out of the barrel of a gun"[10] and emphasized organizing and mobilizing overwhelming masses to fight the enemy. Until Castro came to power, he had not established any major institution and failed to mobilize or organize large-scale operations. It was not until 3 October 1965, when he inaugurated the new Cuban Communist party, that Castro centralized political power and began to monopolize the institutional use of Marxism in Cuba. Fidel had a double-sided rationale for relying on a small scale group to carry on the operations of revolution. First, a small group was better able to remain undetected by Batista's effective secret police. Second, during the long years of struggle, Castro believed that the power base of Batista was so fragile that one major defeat of Batista's military forces would create a snowball effect that would consequently result in the collapse of the old regime. In his bid for the leadership of the organization, Castro used the same institutional philosophy within the NAM structure and relied on a few dedicated and friendly states to support the Cuban position.

In Iran, however, the revolutionary institutions were weak in comparison to those in both Cuba and China. Iranian leaders were neither a homogeneous group and experienced in military engagements (as in Cuba) nor did they have effective institutional skills to mobilize and direct the masses for an extended period in order to work on monumental projects (as in China). The supporters of Ayatollah Khomeini used an informal network to pass his revolutionary message within and outside Iran. Unlike the Chinese, the Iranian revolutionary institutions did not have much time prior to the revolution to become formidable and experienced because the Shah's old regime collapsed much sooner than expected. Interestingly enough, the Shah's quick downfall can be explained by either Mao's or Castro's institutional philosophies. In Mao's terminology, the Shah was just another "paper tiger" who could not withstand the overwhelming popular demonstrations. From Castro's perspective, the Shah's quick overthrow was another example that a small dedicated group of ideologues (i.e., the clergy) could outlive a powerful opponent.

In contrast to the Chinese and Cuban leaders, Iranian leaders faced a dilemma after the revolution. On one hand, they had at their disposal the old institutions which they did not trust: on the other were new institutions established by their followers. Moreover, the start of the Iran-Iraq War did not give Iranian leaders a chance to complete the reorganization of the government. Thus, they established parallel revolutionary institutions alongside the institutions of the old regime. This resulted in duplication and institutional rivalry—two of the major problems of revolutionary Iran. The institutional rivalry contributed to contending policies, and the rival institutions became the cradle for opposing leaders. For example, while the idealists were more influential among the IRGC, the realists came to rely more on the old army. Tehran's failure to build a coalition among contending leaders of the domestic institutions paralleled its shortcomings in building a coalition supporting Iran's bid for leadership of NAM in the 1980s.

Nature of the Foreign Policy

While the non-alignment strategies of revolutionary Cuba and China were secular in nature, Iranian non-alignment had a religious nature. Although Tehran had a legal and political basis for its non-alignment policy, its strategy was primarily founded on an Iranian version of Islam or Shiaism, as analyzed clearly in the previous chapter. Moreover, since Shia theology is a synthesis of Islamic doctrine and Iranian cultural heritage, it can be argued that the non-alignment policy of Revolutionary Iran has a definite cultural basis.

The foreign policy of Revolutionary Cuba was based on the Marxist notion of the struggle against imperialism. There were also other Marxist concepts that affected Cuban non-alignment foreign policy, including economic equality and public ownership. The influence of Marxist economics on Cuban strategy was so significant that one could characterize Havana's foreign policy, especially its non-alignment aspects, as having an economic basis.

The foreign relations of Revolutionary China, however, were oriented more toward political reality than cultural necessity (like Iran) or economic requirement (like Cuba). Although both Beijing and Havana subscribed to Marxism in defining the goals of their foreign policies, it was the political reality of the region that led the People's Republic to alter its ties with both superpowers. Revolutionary China aimed to erase its past political humiliation at the hands of Western Europeans by forcing them out of its territory and by guarding against a possible invasion led by Chiang Kai-shek, who, from the perspective of the Red Chinese, had strong ties with colonial powers. During these politically uncertain days, the Chinese welcomed Moscow's friendship. When the Soviets failed, however, to back Revolutionary China's attempt to liberate Taiwan, Beijing believed it was time to change the nature of its foreign relations with Moscow.

SIMILARITIES IN FOREIGN POLICY STRATEGIES

Although different domestic sources of policy have led to differences among foreign policies of the three revolutionary states, there are considerable similarities in terms of their foreign relations. These are influenced by new public policy initiatives, nationalistic traits, geopolitical factors, foreign policy trends, and strategic lessons learned.

New Public Policy Initiatives

In breaking with the past, the revolutionary regimes of this study were reacting to the domestic as well as foreign policies of their predecessors. Castro, Khomeini, and Mao were opposed to the foreign relations orientations of the previous regimes: their new initiatives would test both superpowers.

From an American perspective, the United States had special relations with all three countries before their respective revolutions. Moreover, on the individual level, American leaders had close personal ties with the leaders of the Chinese, Cuban, and Iranian old regimes that were deposed by the revolutions. Finally, the new revolutionary leaders seemed to use anti-American rhetoric.

While the new initiatives of these regimes had an anti-American flavor, however, it seems doubtful that all revolutionary leaders sought to cut their relations with the United States. This point was illustrated in the three cases as each revolutionary state initially aimed to distance itself from, but not to sever its ties with, Washington. For the American foreign policymakers, however, the changing nature of their relations must have seemed to indicate that they had lost a friend to the Soviets in a zero-sum game.

Interestingly enough, none of these revolutionary states immediately cut off its ties with the United States, even though they were opposed to the main aspects of American foreign policy. Since they felt threatened by U.S. initiatives, their initiatives toward Washington gradually became more conflictual. Although a series of events and not a particular incident often led to a change in the nature of their ties with the United States, it is possible to identify one event that began the chain reaction. In Revolutionary Iran's case, it was the admission of the Shah to America. For Revolutionary China, it was the reaffirmation by the United States that the Chinese Nationalist government was the official representative of all Chinese. And for Revolutionary Cuba, it was the refusal, at the request of the State Department, by American oil companies in Cuba to refine imported Soviet crude.

Moscow's reaction toward the new foreign relations initiatives of these states was different from that of Washington. This created an impression of a more cooperative relationship between these revolutionary regimes and Russia than actually existed. The initial success of Moscow was partly due to its more cautious approach in each case. For example, even in Revolutionary China where the CCP was coming to power, the Soviet Union maintained its ties with Chiang Kai-shek's regime to the last possible moment. In fact, the Russian ambassador was the only diplomatic delegate who accompanied the retreating Nationalist leaders to Canton.[11]

Nationalism

Although the foreign relations of revolutionary China and Cuba were influenced by Marxism and that of Iran by Khomeini's Islamic thought, their policies also showed common signs of nationalism. This was evident in their drive to regain control over their national resources and to protect their territorial integrity. To this end, Revolutionary Iran crushed the Kurdish, Turkman, and Baluchi uprisings in the name of defending the territorial integrity of the state, not in the name of Allah. Additionally, some revolutionary leaders renewed past Iranian claims over the island of Bahrain.

The revolutionary Chinese also showed many nationalistic traits. In fact, the communist Chinese seemed more nationalistic than their predecessor when they began to reassert Beijing's control over China's territory. This included the efforts to bring Tibet and Port Arthur under Chinese administration.[12] Nationalistic aspirations were also the root of its efforts to regain control of Taiwan, Macao, and Hong Kong. Military clashes occurred near the borders of Macao and Hong Kong until Beijing reached understandings with Lisbon and London. Moreover, Revolutionary China moved to regain control over national resources and revoked foreign privileges in its territory. These were tasks that the Nationalists had failed to accomplish.

Similarly inspired by nationalism, Revolutionary Cuba struggled to regain control of the American base at Guantánamo Bay. The control of this base became the main complaint of the Cuban delegates at the Conference of Non-Aligned Countries in 1961. This led NAM to pronounce its opposition to foreign military bases in general and the abolishment of the American base in Cuba in particular.[13]

The foreign relations of these revolutionary states also indicated the influence of geopolitical factors. Geographically, none of the three states was an equal distance from both superpowers. In fact, they were next to one superpower and a long way from the other. Revolutionary China and Iran had long borders with the Soviet Union while they were thousands of miles away from the United States. In this respect, Chinese and Iranian leaders always had to consider the fact of geographic proximity to Russia in their foreign policymaking before and after their revolutions.

Prerevolutionary China hoped to balance the influence of the Russians in the north with that of the other Europeans in the south and vice versa. Although Revolutionary China put the defense of its shoreline high on its agenda, it was also concerned about the unresolved border dispute with Russia. Furthermore, the end of the "lean to one side" strategy paralleled growing Chinese concerns about the renewal of the threat from the north by the Russians. Aiming to deter Moscow, Beijing attempted to create a strategic triangle long before the Kissinger-Nixon period in the 1970s. They did not succeed in establishing ties with Washington, mainly because America did not reciprocate Chinese conciliatory gestures.

For the Islamic Republic of Iran, its geopolitical situation was similar to that of China and led to the setting of similar priorities in its foreign policy agenda. In prerevolutionary Iran, the Shah had altered the traditional strategy of maintaining a balance between the influence of the Russians in the north and the British in the south by aligning Iran with Washington. Like the People's Republic of China, revolutionary Iran first aimed to distance itself from the West, particularly the United States. Its declaration of non-alignment served this particular policy priority.[14] Although Tehran did not formally align itself with Moscow as Beijing had done, the clergy did collaborate with the pro-Soviet Tudeh party. Like the Beijing-Moscow alliance, the Clergy-Tudeh coalition did not last, since the clergy were concerned that its strong anti-American stand might lead to increased influence in its affairs by its northern neighbor, as the Chinese had experienced earlier.

Revolutionary Cuba's geographic situation was slightly different from that of China and Iran, but Havana's ties with Moscow were still a function of its geopolitical situation. Located in the American sphere of influence, Cuba first collaborated with the Russians to possibly deter intervention by the Americans as China and Iran had experienced. The geographic distance from Moscow, however, gave Havana the leeway to maintain close ties with Russia even though it had reservations about Soviet policy. Thus, the foreign relations of the three and their non-alignment strategies were similarly influenced by geopolitical considerations. In short, the nearest superpower was feared the most, regardless of ideology.

Policy Trends

There were also similarities among the three revolutionary regimes in terms of common trends in their foreign policies and the nature of their relations with the Great Powers. The first similarity was that revolutionary China, Cuba, and Iran initially distanced themselves from the United States. Another similarity was that all three came into conflict in the earliest phase of their revolutions with the United States and at the later phase with the Soviet Union. Nevertheless, Moscow was not spared from the sharp edge of the policies of these revolutionary regimes as China (in 1958), Cuba (in 1962), and Iran (in 1982) exhibited. Yet, another similarity was that during the first stage of the postrevolutionary period, foreign policy rhetoric of these regimes tended to be more conflictual than their actual behavior.

Conflictual rhetoric turned into confrontational behavior as the revolutionary leaders of each regime consolidated power. As regime confidence grew in tandem with their successes in consolidating power, the revolutionary regimes projected power more aggressively toward perceived enemies. They began to use force to achieve foreign policy objectives, just as they had done in attaining their domestic goals. Some examples of using force rather than the "due process of law" to implement domestic policies were the speedy trials and executions of Chinese landowners by the PLA and the distribution of their land among the peasants; Castro's nationalization of the property of American citizens in Cuba without paying adequate compensation; and Iran's forceful confiscation of many private banks, companies, large factories, and other personal property in the name of the revolution.

The three revolutionary regimes resorted to force in various forms, ranging from war to subversion. China expanded the scope of the Korean War by directly entering that conflict. The Chinese also provided some assistance to national liberation movements throughout Southeast Asia. Revolutionary Cuba initiated an international crisis by obtaining long-range missiles from the Soviets in 1962. Another significant sign of Cuba's confrontational posture was its economic and military assistance to guerilla and revolutionary movements throughout Latin America in the post-missile crisis era. Revolutionary Iran also pursued a bellicose course of action similar to that of China and Cuba. In 1979, radical students stormed the U.S. Embassy, held American diplomats hostage, and scrutinized and selectively published classified U.S. Embassy documents. This act was not only against Washington, but also against the whole international community. This action showed defiance of the world order since one of the fundamental principles of international law—diplomatic immunity—had been directly violated.[15] Moreover, Iran's leaders moved the war into Iraqi territory in 1982, raising the level of hostilities. Additionally, during the more conflictual stage of their foreign relations, Iranian revolutionary idealists, like their Chinese and Cuban counterparts, aided opposition forces throughout the region in an attempt to destabilize other governments.

In all three cases, however, the confrontational nature of the foreign policies of the revolutionary regimes gradually limited the diplomatic, economic, and military contacts with some powers and often led to reliance on other states. Consequently, the revolutionary regimes, in effect, limited their diplomatic options and room for maneuvering. As a result, they increased their dependence on fewer states. Revolutionary China and Cuba found themselves dependent on Moscow's economic and technological assistance. For Iran, however, the situation was somewhat different. Tehran did not depend on Soviet economic aid, but it did count on Moscow's diplomatic assistance to defuse Washington's initiative in the U.N. Security Council, at least until Resolution 598 was passed. It is important to mention that throughout this period, Iran's only dependence was on American technology for its military machine. The prolonged war with Iraq proved this point to Tehran, despite the significant growth of the domestic military industry in Iran.[16]

As the revolutionary states ran out of steam, they began to show signs of more conciliatory diplomacy, especially toward the Great Powers. China was more willing to negotiate when the Korean War became a burden on the national economy. Similarly, when the burden of the war became overwhelming, Iranian revolutionary leaders found it necessary to have some constructive contacts with the "Great Satan." As chapter 5 indicated, during the Iran-Contra Affair even revolutionary idealists opened a channel of communication with the Americans, as the efforts of Ghorbanifar illustrated. The Revolutionary Cubans also had a similar experience. As the cost of the isolation period became too high for the regime to bear, Havana began to soften its foreign policy conduct by putting more emphasis on government-to-government relations than ties with the liberation movements, as discussed in chapter 4.

While the foreign policy orientations of Cuba and Iran became more conciliatory in nature, this change did not manifest itself until the revolutionary regimes failed to meet the national challenges for which they had mobilized their national resources. For Havana, the national challenge was meeting the sugar quota, while for Iran, it was capturing Basra.

In China's case, the situation was somewhat different. The national challenge—the Great Leap Forward—had actually begun during the more conciliatory stage of Chinese foreign policy. The disastrous results of the Great Leap Forward campaign could have resulted in improved ties with the superpowers since the Chinese would have needed to secure more international assistance for their modernization efforts. The posturing of the superpowers, however, during an incident in China's more conciliatory stage resulted in China's withdrawal from its conciliatory position to one that was resentful, isolationist, and eventually confrontational. This significant incident was the Offshore Island Crisis, during which the People's Republic of China felt deserted by Moscow. The People's Republic was counting on Russian diplomatic and material support during this conflict with Taiwan. The Soviets, however, had no interest in assisting China in what they considered to be an ambitious plan to gain control of Taiwan. At the same time that Beijing felt betrayed by its superpower friend, it also saw that the Americans were unyielding in their support of the Taiwanese.

LESSONS LEARNED

Although the three states exhibited some differences in conducting their foreign relations based on a non-alignment strategy, it appears that they learned similar lessons. The first lesson was that the Great Powers dominated the international system, like it or not. Given this political reality, regional conflict was redefined in terms of the global interests of the superpowers. For Beijing, the Korean War and the offshore islands crisis were cases in point. From Revolutionary China's perspective, the American involvement in Korea was a regional nuisance, but at least the Soviets supported the Chinese efforts in the Korean War. The offshore islands crisis, however, was another matter.

For Havana, the missile crisis was an example of a superpower imposing its will on a small state. From Havana's perspective, the request for the Russian missiles was an attempt to deter another Bay-of-Pigs-style American invasion even though Moscow may have had other goals. And for Tehran, the Iran-Iraq War became a regional crisis fueled by both superpowers who tacitly opposed a decisive Iranian victory.

The second lesson was the realization that they had limited capabilities to deal with a major crisis. Although Beijing had the necessary manpower to devote to the offshore islands crisis, Revolutionary China's forces did not have the technological edge over their Taiwanese counterparts. Furthermore, the direct involvement of Washington in this crisis had neutralized the advantage of size that Beijing's forces had over Taipei's forces. Similarly, the missile crisis taught Havana that Cuba's actual capability and its "borrowed capacity"[17] were limited. Thus, Havana learned that if Washington perceived a local development in Cuba as being dangerous to American national security, it would intervene in order to neutralize the source of the threat and deter the potential enemy, even if it were Moscow.

Revolutionary Iran learned that its highly devoted followers were no match for the well-equipped Iraqi forces, who had both the blessing and support of the superpowers in their containment of Iranian revolutionary fervor. Despite their rhetoric, Iranian leaders realized that their forces were no match for those of either superpower on a battlefield. In this respect, Tehran was convinced of the effectiveness of the American forces, after the U.S.–Iran engagement in the Persian Gulf during 1987 and 1988. Iran also learned through its joint operation with Afghan allies that the Russians were a formidable enemy in the battle zone. Finally, Tehran discovered that its dedicated forces could not even break through the defensive line of the Iraqis in order to capture any major city.

The third lesson was that by adopting a rigid confrontational stance, a revolutionary state could effectively limit its policy options in a crisis. In fact, Revolutionary Cuba, which initiated an international crisis by requesting long-range missiles, did not have any say in the negotiations that ended the crisis simply because Moscow ignored Havana's input. Like the Cubans, the Chinese did not have many policy options without the support of the Russians. This was particularly evident when Washington began directly assisting the Taiwanese during the offshore islands crisis. Under such conditions, all the Chinese could do was to look for a face-saving formula to end the crisis before it reached the point of no return.

Iran also faced limited options because of its rigid non-alignment posture. Iranian non-alignment succeeded in assisting the revolutionary regime's fierce sense of independence from Moscow or Washington, but Iran's intransigence united the superpowers in opposing a possible Iranian victory in the war with Iraq. This union obviously limited Tehran's options in ending the war on its own terms and left the acceptance of U.N. Security Council Resolution 598 as the only rational option for The Islamic Republic. Thus, in effect, an internationally imposed peace seemed to end what the Iranians called "the imposed war."

SOME OBSERVATIONS ABOUT NON-ALIGNMENT STRATEGIES

This study shows that the concept of non-alignment, defined as the absence of leaning toward, or aligning with, a superpower, may actually manifest itself in different ways. The five non-alignment criteria described in chapter 2 are conducive to differences since the criteria are rather general and somewhat vague. Contrary to conventional wisdom, a non-aligned country, whether revolutionary or not may choose to have closer ties with one superpower. Or, it may even temporarily collaborate with one superpower, not necessarily against the other superpower, but to protect its interests. To maintain genuine non-alignment, however, a non-aligned country should not, by the same criterion, permanently remain in a dependent position vis-à-vis one particular Great Power. This concern led Havana to change the nature of its ties with Moscow from dependence to interdependence.

In a slightly different situation, the Chinese gradually shifted from a vague alignment to a vocal and de facto non-alignment posture in their foreign relations. Considering the regional political conditions at the time, Cuba and China seemed to have made a rational choice to initially align themselves with Moscow while they felt threatened about the survival of their revolutionary regimes. For instance, the Revolutionary Chinese leaders were seriously concerned about Chiang Kaishek's promise that he would return. In fact, this promise had led to several rumors of the possible invasion of mainland China on its vulnerable southern shores. That was why close association with the Russians made sense at the beginning, but they moved away from Moscow's orbit when they felt more confident about the survival of their regime.

The nature and trend of Iranian relations with the superpowers indicated still another application of non-alignment. Tehran succeeded in allowing its revolution to be defined in compliance with the exigencies of the East-West confrontation. Moreover, unlike the Chinese and Cubans, the Iranians avoided having closer ties with Moscow in an effort to prevent direct American intervention in their affairs. After all, American concerns about the increasing influence of the Marxist Tudeh party in the Mossadegh government led the United States to design and direct the 1953 coup and return the Shah to power. Moreover, considering the geographic proximity of the two states, a Tehran–Moscow alignment could have reversed the regional balance of forces that favored Washington and could possibly have led to a stronger U.S. reaction toward Revolutionary Iran. Thus, Tehran's strict non-alignment strategy was also a rational decision, considering the vital strategic value of the region for the West, particularly the United States. Washington was quite concerned that a hostile state controlling the traffic through the Strait of Hormuz could use Western energy vulnerability to its own advantage. In fact, this concern led the United States to carefully watch Soviet moves in the Persian Gulf region.[18]

In opposition to the views of some critics, a workable non-alignment strategy was not merely the result of wishful thinking. It required using realpolitik to achieve policy goals. This does not mean that all non-aligned states successfully utilized a prudent approach in their foreign relations at all times. For instance, Revolutionary Iran is a country that neglected to accept the significance of realpolitik in posturing itself between the superpowers. When a confrontation with Washington seemed unavoidable (or even beneficial), instead of using realpolitik or playing his Moscow card, Ayatollah Khomeini chose to directly confront the "Great Satan" by approving, ipso facto, the takeover of the American Embassy. Also on other occasions, Revolutionary Iran refused to use its Moscow card by rejecting Russia's attempts to mediate both the hostage crisis and the Iran-Iraq War. Thus, Iran's persistence in keeping its revolution out of the East-West conflict led to a rigid non-alignment posture. Unlike revolutionary China and Cuba, The Islamic Republic did not benefit from the rivalry between the two superpowers, mainly due to its strict non-alignment posture.

Non-alignment was not only a goal, but was also a means for achieving a significant end. In this respect, the common denominator of all three states was that their non-alignment policies were a means of protecting their revolutions. The revolutionary leaders in China, Cuba, and Iran opposed foreign control and believed that it was the source of all evil in their countries. The revolutionaries' promises of a better future and a return of lost national pride were to be achieved by improving domestic socioeconomic conditions as well as by resisting foreign control. Since Western powers were regarded as behaving like colonial powers, fighting against Western domination was perceived as a just cause. From this perspective, the revolutionary regimes were as much for independence as they were against the domestic injustices of their predecessors. In fact, their non-aligned foreign relations strategies can be explained by their strong commitments to independence. Although none of these states in the prerevolutionary era were a full-fledged colony, their revolutionary movements succeeded in portraying the old regimes of the Shah, Batista, and Chiang Kai-shek as dependent upon imperialism and symbols of colonialism. In this context, the revolutionary leaders boasted that the revolutions had given a new life to their old states and provided true independence and freedom from foreign control. Thus, protecting the revolutions was the ultimate goal of the non-alignment strategies, which began in all three cases by treating the superpowers unequally.

If, however, their non-alignment policies were to be considered genuine, how should one account for the period when these states maintained uneven relations with the superpowers? In response to this question, it is critical to note that, contrary to popular belief, the practice of non-alignment does not necessarily mean equal relations with both superpowers. Additionally, regarding the notions of equal and independent, a parallel may be drawn between the approaches of non-alignment and separation of powers. That is, the separation of powers does not mean that the three branches of government are physically equal, but it does mean that they are independent from control by the other powers. Similarly, non-alignment does not necessarily mean equal relations with (or treatment of) both superpowers. In fact, a non-aligned state may choose to maintain any form of relations with a superpower (short of a military alliance against the other superpower) that helps it remain an independent political unit in the international community.

Theoretically, it is possible to assume that a state can treat the superpowers equally and remain indifferent toward them both. In practice, however, one does not treat friend and foe equally. Although most Third World states seemed equally enthusiastic about non-alignment, they often have a more cooperative relationship with one or the other superpowers. In this study, the cooperative stance was usually with the superpower that presented the least amount of danger to the state's independence. Since the United States was the symbolic target of the revolutions in China, Cuba, and Iran, the new regimes did not even begin by treating the superpowers equally. The initial positive attitude of these states toward Moscow, though, did not pass the test of time.

The initial cooperative gestures of these revolutionary states toward the

Russians had a commonsense basis. Beyond the rhetoric of the Soviets as the older, ideological brother or ally in the struggle against Western imperialism, the Russians offered extensive economic and technical assistance to both revolutionary China and Cuba. The West, on the other hand, had abandoned them after their revolutions. Moscow also offered assistance to Iran, but Tehran's main demand remained the Soviet withdrawal of military supplies to Iraq during the war. For the most part, the Russians complied with this request until the clergy broke its alliance with the Tudeh party and began to purge the pre-Soviet political party in Iran.

By accepting Soviet aid, both China and Cuba eased the difficulties associated with their modernization efforts during the initial years of their revolutions. Furthermore, they each had a Moscow card to play against Washington, should it be necessary. In contrast, Iran did it the hard way by insisting on neither an East nor West policy that, in practice, meant no friendly superpowers to assist it when needed. Therefore, the price of a genuine and rigid non-alignment posture in foreign relations was high for Tehran.

Moreover, Beijing and Havana did not perceive that they had restricted their freedom of action by accepting Soviet aid because the nature of the prerevolutionary presence of the Russians was very different from that of the Western powers. This difference was highlighted by Castro, who said that the Americans owned his country while the Russians did not own anything in Revolutionary Cuba.

Did the acceptance of Soviet aid, in fact, put the Chinese or Cubans in a subservient position vis-à-vis the Russians? This study did not confirm such a conclusion and showed that occasionally revolutionary China and Cuba either initiated international campaigns that opposed the interests of Moscow or they did not respond to certain events according to the expectations of the Russians. Furthermore, when the Chinese and the Cubans began to fear that their independent foreign policymaking could be compromised by relying on Moscow, each came up with a different solution to the problem. China began to distance itself from the Soviet Union, just it they had done earlier from the United States. The Cubans, however, protected their independence by creating a mutually interdependent relationship with the Russians. In fact, as Moscow began to depend more on Havana to bring the Third World closer to the Second World position, they were less likely to infringe on Cuban independence as long as Havana was not involving Moscow in a major international crisis as it did in 1962.

While all Third World states want to protect their independence, they also realize that independence is a matter of degree. All strategies to protect the independence of a Third World state fall on an alignment/non-alignment continuum. The degree of alignment or non-alignment provided advantages suited to the state's particular domestic or international agenda. For example, a Third World state may have chosen alignment with the First or the Second World because it perceives itself as too weak to withstand an external threat or because it realized that its strategic situation was too significant for the superpowers to leave it alone. In either case, the Third World state understands that its weakness will create a dependence on its strongest ally. This dependence, however, is a price that it may be willing to pay in order to protect its survival and to maintain some degree of autonomy.

In contrast to those Third World states that opt for alignment, the non-aligned states are a group with more diverse goals. Some wanted to maintain their role as buffer or neutral states in certain geographic regions, like Afghanistan in the Middle East and Laos in Southeast Asia. Others were not strategically significant to the superpowers, who consequently did not exert pressure on them to align. Most non-aligned African states that are not strategically significant (except Egypt, Ethiopia, and Morocco) fall into this category.

Another attraction for many Third World states to join NAM may have been the idea that there was safety in numbers. This idea, however, did not accurately describe the intention of a few, like India, to join NAM. This was due to India's being strong enough to remain secure on its own despite the superpower rivalry. There were also some states, like Indonesia, that found the international conditions suitable for securing foreign assistance from both ideological blocs. Nevertheless, most Third World states found that a strategy of non-alignment met the needs of their domestic, more than their international, affairs. This statement is particularly appropriate for the three revolutionary regimes discussed here.

In sum, pursuing non-alignment in foreign relations is about maintaining political independence from others, particularly the Great Powers. To maintain a separate identity, the non-aligned state might temporarily coordinate diplomatic activities with one Great Power on issues of mutual interest. The ultimate objective of a Third World state, however, remains its independence or freedom from foreign interference in the policymaking process. Among Third World countries, the drives of the revolutionary states toward independence seems to be the strongest largely in order to ensure the survival of their revolutions in the face of a hostile international environment. Thus, for the three states in particular, and the Third World in general, non-alignment serves as a means for maintaining a separate identity and remaining autonomous in an increasingly interdependent world.

NOTES

1. The quality of life indicators such as adult literacy and life expectancy were lower even for prerevolutionary Iran in comparison with China and Cuba. See The World Bank, *World Development Report 1981* (New York: Oxford University Press, 1981).

2. Ibid, 134.

3. For an analysis of Cuban income distribution, see Claes Brudenius, *Revolutionary Cuba: The Challenge of Economic Growth with Equity* (Boulder, Colo. Westview Press, 1984), 105-18. For a comparative discussion of Cuban economic growth and equity, see the same source, pp. 119-24.

4. For comparing the military strength of the three states during the heyday of the Shah's military might, see *World Armaments and Disarmament: SIPRI Yearbook* (Cambridge: MIT Press for Stockholm International Peace Research Institute, 1976). Also see International

Institute for Strategic Studies, *The Military Balance, 1978–1979* (London: International Institute for Strategic Studies, 1978). For a comparison of the three states during the first decade of Revolutionary Iran, see *SIPRI Yearbook* (1990).

5. Haleh Afshar, ed., *Iran: A Revolution in Turmoil* (Albany: State University of New York Press, 1985).

6. Even this projection was questionable as far as Saudi Arabia was concerned because Riyadh had sufficient means to deter Tehran, as demonstrated by their air engagement incidents of 5 June 1984. See R. K. Ramazani, *Revolutionary Iran: Challenge and Response in the Middle East* rev. ed. (Baltimore, Md.: Johns Hopkins University Press, 1988), 9.

7. For biographical information that covers Chinese communist figures, see Donald Klein and Anne B. Clark, *Biographical Dictionary of Chinese Communism, 1921–1965*, 2 vols. (Cambridge: Harvard University Press, 1970). For a more general treatment of the main leaders, see Robert S. Elegant, *China's Red Masters: Political Biographies of the Chinese Communist Leaders* (Westport, Conn.: Greenwood Press, 1971). For a history of modern China based on a series of biographies, see Jonathan D. Spence, *The Gate of Heavenly Peace* (New York: Viking, 1981).

8. Even at the height of Sino–Soviet friendship, Chinese leaders were not reticent in emphasizing the very serious differences that had punctuated the early history of the relationship between the two parties; see "More on the Historical Experience of Proletarian Dictatorship," translated in *Supplement to People's China* 2, no. 16 (January 1957): 10. For an analysis of the uneasy relations between the Russian and Chinese communist leaders, see Robert C. North, *Moscow and the Chinese Communists* (Stanford, Calif.: Stanford University Press, 1953).

9. For a discussion of the background, role, and leadership of Castro, see Herbert L. Matthews, *Fidel Castro* (New York: Simon and Schuster, 1969).

10. *Quotations From Chairman Mao Tse-tung* (Peking: Foreign Languages Press, 1966).

11. Alan Lawrance, *China's Foreign Relations Since 1949* (London: Routledge and Kegan Paul, 1975), 22.

12. On Chinese attempts to regain Port Arthur, see Joseph Camilleri, *Chinese Foreign Policy: The Maoist Era and Its Aftermath* (Oxford: Martin Robertson, 1980), 49.

13. Rozita Levi, "Cuba and the Nonaligned Movement," in *Cuba in the World* eds. Cole Blasier and Carmelo Mesa-Lago (Pittsburgh: University of Pittsburgh Press, 1979), 148.

14. This is not to deny that from an ideological perspective, non alignment strategy was a rejection of a world order determined by the superpowers. On the rejection of the international order according to the views of Ayatollah Khomeini, see Ramazani, 19-21.

15. For a discussion of the significance of diplomatic immunity, see Gerhard von Glahn, *Law Among Nations*, 3d ed. (New York: Macmillan, 1976), especially pp. 386-94.

16. On the general condition of the Iranian military following the revolution, see Helen Metz, ed., *Iran: A Country Study* (Washington, D.C.: U.S. Government Printing Office, 1989), 238-71 and 279-98.

17. This concept, coined by R. K. Ramazani, in this context, means the Soviet power supporting Cuba. The borrowed capacity, however, was not enough to give the Cubans the winning advantage for the Russians backed down in facing superior American forces. In fact, after the crisis, Moscow began a major military buildup to match the quality of the U.S. forces (John T. Rourke, *International Politics on the World Stage*, 3d ed. (Guilford, Conn.: Dushkin Publishing Group, 1991), 45.

18. For a discussion of the challenges to American policy in the Persian Gulf, see Thomas Perry Thornton, *The Challenge to U.S. Policy in the Third World* (Boulder, Colo.: Westview Press, 1986), especially pp. 85-95.

SELECTED BIBLIOGRAPHY

Agency for International Development. *U.S. Overseas Loans and Grants.* Washington D.C.: U.S. Government Printing Office, 1990.

Allison, Graham T. *Essence of Decision.* Boston: Little, Brown, 1971.

Allison, R. *The Soviet Union and the Strategy of Non-Alignment in the Third World.* Cambridge: Cambridge University Press, 1988.

Armstrong, J. D. *Revolutionary Diplomacy: Chinese Foreign Policy and the United Front Doctrine.* Berkeley: University of California Press, 1977.

Babbitt, Irving. *Rousseau and Romanticism.* Boston: Houghton Mifflin, 1947.

Baehr, Peter R. and Leon Gordenker. *The United Nations in the 1990s,* 2d ed. New York: St. Martin's Press, 1994.

Bakhash, S. *The Reign of the Ayatollahs,* rev. ed. New York: Basic Books, 1986.

Bailyn, Bernard. *The Ideological Origins of the American Revolution.* Cambridge, Mass.: Harvard University Press, 1967.

Bajpai, U.S. *Non-Alignment: Perspectives and Prospects.* New Delhi: Lancers Publishers, 1983.

Belovski, D. "The Activities and Aims of Yugoslavia as a Non-Aligned and Socialist Country." *Review of International Affairs* 21, no. 480 (1970): 3-6.

Bianco, Lucien. *Origins of the Chinese Revolution 1915–1949.* Stanford: Stanford University Press, 1967.

Bill, James. "The New Iran: Relations with its Neighbors and the United States." *Asian Update* (August 1991), pp. 3-13.

Birnbaum, K. E. and H. P. Neuhold, eds. *Neutrality and Non-Alignment in Europe.* Vienna: Braumuller, 1981.

Blagovic, Bozica. "The Ideological and Political Foundations of Non-Alignment." *Review of International Affairs* 32, nos. 752-753 (5-20 August 1981): 5-8.

Blasier, Cole and Carmelo Mesa-Lago, eds. *Cuba in the World.* Pittsburgh: University of Pittsburgh Press, 1979.

Blix, H. *Sovereignty, Aggression, and Neutrality.* (Uppsala, Sweden: 1970).

Bonsal, Philip. *Cuba, Castro and the United States.* Pittsburgh: University of Pittsburgh Press, 1971).

Brenner, Philip. *From Confrontation to Negotiation: U.S. Relations with Cuba.* Boulder, Colo.: Westview Press, 1988).

Brewitt-Taylor, C. H., trans. *Romance of the Three Kingdoms.* Oxford: Oxford University Press, 1925.

Brinton, Crane. *The Anatomy of Revolution.* New York: Vintage Books, 1965.

Brown, Macalister and Joseph J. Zasloff. *Apprentice Revolutionaries: The Communist Movement in Laos, 1930–1985.* Stanford, Calif.: Hoover Institute, Stanford University Press, 1986.

Brudenius, Claes. *Revolutionary Cuba: The Challenge of Economic Growth with Equity.* Boulder, Colo.: Westview Press, 1984.

Brugger, Bill. *China: Radicalism to Revisionism, 1962–1979.* London: Croom Helm, Ltd., 1981.

Buchan, Alastair. "Bipolarity and Coalition." *Pacific Community.* 5 no. 3 (April 1974): 348-62.

Burchett, Wilfred. *The China–Cambodia–Vietnam Triangle.* London: Zed Books, 1981.

Camilleri, Joseph. *Chinese Foreign Policy: The Maoist Era and its Aftermath.* Oxford: Martin Robertson & Company, 1980.

Chang, Gordon H. *Friends and Enemies: The United States, China, and the Soviet Union, 1948–1972.* Stanford, Calif.: Stanford University Press, 1990.

Chawla, S., M. Gurtov, and A. Marsot, eds. *Southeast Asia Under the New Balance of Power.* New York: Praeger, 1974.

Chen, Jian. *The Sino–Soviet Alliance and China's Entry into the Korean War.* Washington, D.C.: Cold War International History Project, Woodrow Wilson International Center for Scholars, 1992.

Ch'en Kung-po. *The Communist Movement in China.* New York: Columbia University Press, 1960.

Cima, Ronald J., ed. *Vietnam: A Country Study.* Washington, D.C.: United States Government Publishing Office, 1989.

Claude, Inis L., Jr. *Power and International Relations.* New York: Random House, 1962.
———. *Swords into Plowshares,* 4th ed. New York: Random House, 1984.

Cohen, Warren I. *America's Response to China: A History of Sino-American Relations,* 3d ed. New York: Columbia University Press, 1990.

Connell-Smith, Gordon. *The Inter-American System.* New York: Oxford University Press, 1966.

Cottam, R. W. *Iran and the United States.* Pittsburgh: University of Pittsburgh Press, 1988.

Dahl, Robert. *After the Revolution?: Authority in a Good Society.* New Haven, Conn.: Yale University Press, 1970.

Dittmer, Lowell. *Liu-Shao-ch'i and the Chinese Cultural Revolution.* Berkeley: University of California Press, 1974.

Dominguez, Jorge I., ed. *Cuba: Internal and International Affairs.* Beverly Hills, Calif.: Sage Publications, 1982.

Dominguez, Jorge I. *Cuba: Order and Revolution.* Cambridge: Harvard University Press, Belknap Press, 1978.

Dougherty, James E. and Robert L. Pfaltzgraff, Jr. *Contending Theories of International Relations,* 3d ed. New York: Harper and Row, 1990.

Duiker, William J. *China and Vietnam: The Roots of Conflict.* Berkeley: University of California Press, Institute of East Asia Studies, 1986.

Dunn, John. *Modern Revolutions.* Cambridge: University Press of Cambridge: 1972.
———. *Modern Revolutions,* 2nd ed. Cambridge: Cambridge University Press, 1989.

Edwards, Lyford P. *The Natural History of Revolution*. Chicago: University of Chicago Press, 1927. First published in 1927.

Erisman, Michael. *Cuba's International Relations*. Boulder: Westview Press, 1985.

Farrell, Barry, ed. *Approaches to Comparative and International Politics*. Evanston, Ill.: Northwestern University Press, 1966.

Farsi, Jalal Al-Din. *Hoqoq-e Biy Al-Milal-e Islami* [Islamic International Law] Tehran: Intisharat-e Jahan Ara, 136? [198?].

Fauriol, Georges, ed. *Latin American Insurgencies*. Washington, D.C.: The National Defense University Press, 1985.

Fogel, Daniel. *Africa in Struggle: National Liberation and Proletarian Revolution*, 2nd ed. San Francisco: Ism Press, 1986.

Frei, Daniel. "Neutrality." *World Encyclopedia of Peace*. Edited by Linus Pauling. Oxford: Pergamon Press, 1986.

Friedman, Herbert C. *Politics and Mind: Indian Book of International Affairs II*. Madras, India, 1952.

Garson, Robert. *The United States and China Since 1949, A Troubled Affair*. Madison Teanek, United Kingdom: Fairleigh Dickinson University Press, 1994.

Garver, John W. *Chinese-Soviet Relations, 1937–1945*. New York: Oxford University Press, 1988.

Gittings, John. *The Role of the Chinese Army*. London: Oxford University Press, 1967.
———. *The World and China 1922–1972*. New York: Harper and Row, 1974.

Goncharov, Sergei N., John W. Lewis, and Xue Litai. *Uncertain Partners: Stalin, Mao, and the Korean War*. Stanford, Calif.: Stanford University Press, 1993.

Gong, Gerrit. *U.S. China Policy: Building a New Consensus*. Washington, D.C.: The Center for Strategic and International Studies, 1994.

Goodrich, L. M. and D. A. Kay, eds. *International Organization: Politics and Process*. Madison: The University of Wisconsin Press, 1973.

Gopal, Krishan. *Non-Alignment and Power Politics*. New Delhi: V. I. Publications, 1983.

Greene, Fred, ed. *The Philippine Bases: Negotiating for the Future*. New York: Council of Foreign Relations, 1988.

Griffith, Samuel B., II. *The Chinese People's Liberation Army*. New York: McGraw-Hill, 1967.

Hakovirta, H. "The Soviet Union and the Varieties of Neutrality in Europe." *World Politics* 35, no. 4 (1983): 563-85.

Harris, Lillian Craig and Robert L. Worden, eds. *China and the Third World: Champion or Challenger?* Dover, Mass.: Auburn House, 1986.

Hartford, Kathleen and Steven M. Goldstein, eds. *Single Sparks*. Armonk, N.Y.: M. E. Sharpe, 1989.

Hashmi, Zia H. *Iran, Pakistan, and Turkey: Regional Integration and Economic Development*. Lahore, Pakistan: Aziz Publishers, 1979.

Hinton, Harold C. *Communist China in World Politics*. London: Macmillan, 1966.

Hobbes, Thomas. *Leviathan*. Indianapolis: Bobbs-Merrill, 1958.

Holsti, Ole R., P. Terrence Hopmann, and John D. Sullivan. *Unity and Disintegration in International Alliance*. New York: Wiley, 1973.

Horowitz, Irving, Josue DeCastro, and John Gerassi, eds. *Latin American Radicalism*. New York: Random House, 1969.

Hovet, T., Jr. *Bloc Politics in the United Nations*. Cambridge: Harvard University Press, 1960.

Hunter, S. T. *Iran and the World: Continuity in a Revolutionary Decade*. Bloomington:

Indiana University Press, 1990.

Jackson, D. Bruce. *Castro, the Kremlin, and Communism in Latin America.* Baltimore, Md.: Johns Hopkins University Press, 1969.

Jackson, Richard L. *The Non-Aligned, the UN, and the Superpowers.* New York: Praeger, 1983.

Jakobson, M. *Finnish Neutrality.* London: 1969.

Jalal, Al-Ahmad. *Gharbzadeqi* [Westoxication], reprint. Solon, Ohio: Union of Societies of Islamic Students, 1979.

Jan, Y. "We Support the Just Struggle of the Non-Aligned Countries." *Review of International Affairs* 30, no. 692 (5 February 1979): 4-6.

Jankowitsch, O. and K. P. Sauvant, eds. *The Third World Without Superpowers: The Collected Documents of the Non-Aligned Countries.* New York: Oceana, 1978.

Jiang, Arnold Xiangze. *The United States and China.* Chicago: University of Chicago Press, 1988.

Johnson, Chalmors. *Revolutionary Change.* Stanford, Calif.: Stanford University Press, 1966.

Johnson, Loch K. *America as a World Power.* New York: McGraw-Hill, 1991.

Johnston, William C. *Burma's Foreign Policy: A Study in Neutralism.* Cambridge: Harvard University Press, 1963.

Jordan, Robert S., ed. *Dag Hammarskjöld Revisited.* Durham: Carolina Academic Press, 1983.

Jutte, R., ed. *Future Prospects of International Organization.* London: Frances Printer, 1981.

Kardelji, Edvard. "Historical Roots of Non-Alignment." *Bulletin of Peace Proposals* 7, no. 1 (1976): 84-89.

Karnes, Thomas L., ed. *Readings in the Latin American Policy of the United States.* Tucson: University of Arizona Press, 1972.

Karol, K. S. *Guerrillas In Power: The Course of the Cuban Revolution.* New York: Hill and Wang, 1970.

Karunakaran, K. P. "Non-Aligned Radicals." *Seminar,* no. 45 (May 1963): 17-22.

Keating, P. *A Singular Stance: Irish Neutrality in the 1980s.* Dublin: Institute of Public Administration, 1984.

Keddie, Nikki R., ed. *Neither East Nor West.* New Haven, Conn.: Yale University Press, 1990.

Kegly, Charles W., Jr., and Eugene R. Wittkopf, eds. *The Domestic Sources of American Foreign Policy: Insights and Évidence.* New York: St. Martin's Press, 1988.

Keith, Ronald C. *The Diplomacy of Zhou Enlai.* New York: St. Martin's Press, 1989.

Kennedy, Robert F. *Thirteen Days: A Memoir of the Cuban Missile Crisis.* New York: W.W. Norton, 1969.

Kenner, Martin and James Petras, eds. *Fidel Castro Speaks.* New York: Grove Press, 1969.

Khaduri, Majid. *War & Peace in the Law of Islam.* Baltimore: Johns Hopkins University Press, 1985.

Khalilian, Khalil. *Hoqoq-e Biy Al-Milal-e Islami* [Islamic International Law] vol. 1. Tehran: Office of Publications of Islamic Culture, 1362 (1983).

Kim, Samuel, ed. *China and the World,* 2d ed. Boulder, Colo.: Westview Press, 1989.

Kirthisinghe, B. "Non-Alignment Is Not Neutralism." *Modern Review* 123, no. 4 (April 1968): 235-38.

Kissinger, Henry *Years of Upheaval.* Boston: Little, Brown, 1982.

Kitts, Charles R. *The United States Odyssey in China, 1784–1990.* Lanham, Md.: University

Press of America, 1991.

LaFeber, Walter. *America, Russia, and the Cold War, 1945–1990*, 6th ed. New York: McGraw-Hill, 1991.

Lawrance, Alan. *China's Foreign Relations Since 1949*. London: Routledge and Kegan Paul, 1975.

Levesque, Jacques. *The USSR and the Cuban Revolution*. New York: Praeger Special Series, 1978.

Liu, Zuecheng. *The Sino-Indian Border Dispute and Sino-Indian Relations*, Lanham, Md.: University Press of America, 1994.

MacFarguhar, Roderick. *The Hundred Flowers Campaign and the Chinese Intellectuals*. New York: Octagon, 1973.

Mackerras, Colin. *Modern China: A Chronology from 1842 to the Present*. London: Thames and Hudson, 1982.

———. *Western Images of China*. Oxford: Oxford University Press, 1989.

Madsen, Richard. *China and the American Dream: A Moral Inquiry*. Berkeley: University of California Press, 1995.

Malhotra, I. "Non-Alignment: The Indian Approach." *Indian Calling* (July 1976).

Mansori, J. *Farhang-e Isteglal* [The Culture of Independence]. Tehran: Ministry of Foreign Affairs, 1987.

Mao Zedong. *Selected Works of Mao Tse-Tung*, vols. 1-4. Peking: Foreign Languages Press, 1969.

Mates, Leo. "Non-Alignment and the Great Powers." *Foreign Affairs* 48 (1970): 526-36.

———. *Non-Alignment: Theory and Current Policy*. Belgrade: Oceana Publication, 1972.

Matthews, Herbert L. *Revolution in Cuba*. New York: Scribner's, 1975.

Metz, Helen, ed. *Iran: A Country Study*. Washington, D.C.: U.S. Government Printing Office, 1989.

Misra, K. P. "Non-Alignment: A Dynamic Concept." *Indian and Foreign Review* 12, no. 21 (15 August 1975): 11-12.

Modelski, George. *SEATO: Six Studies*. Melbourne, Australia: F.W. Cheshire, 1962.

Mohammadi, M. *Osol-e Siyasat-e Khareji-e Jomhori-e Islami-e Iran* [The Principles of the Foreign Policy of the Islamic Republic of Iran]. Tehran: Amir Kabir, 1987.

Murray, Brian. *Stalin, the Cold War, and the Division of China: A Multi-Archival Mystery*. Washington D.C.: Cold War International History Project, Woodrow Wilson International Center for Scholars, 1995.

Myrdal, Alva. *Asian Drama: An Inquiry into the Poverty of Nations*. Harmondsworth, N.Y.: Penguin, 1968.

———.*The Game of Disarmament: How the United States and Russia Run the Arms Race*. New York: Pantheon Books, 1976.

Narasimha, Rao. "Adherence to the Principles and Aims of Non-Alignment." *Review of International Affairs* 31, no. 724 (5 June 1980): 1-6.

Nehru, Jawaharlal. *India's Foreign Policy*. New Delhi: Government of India Publication Division, 1961.

Nelsen, Harvey W. *Power and Insecurity: Beijing, Moscow, and Washington, 1949–1988*. Boulder, Colo.: Lynne Rienner, 1989.

Neuhold, H.P. "Permanent Neutrality in Contemporary International Relations." *Irish Studies International Affairs* 1, no. 3 (1982): 13-26.

Nikezic, M. "Why Uncommitted Countries Hold That They Are Non Neutral." *Annals of the American Academy of Political and Social Science* 336 (July 1961): 75-82.

North, Robert C. *Moscow and the Chinese Communists*. Stanford, Calif.: Stanford

University Press, 1953.

Ogden, Suzanne. *China.* Global Studies Series, 4th ed. vol. 12. Guilford, CT: The Dushkin Publishing Group, 1991.

———. *China's Unresolved Issues: Politics, Development, and Culture*, 3d ed. Englewood Cliffs, N.J.: Prentice-Hall, 1995.

Ogley, R. *The Theory and Practice of Neutrality in the Twentieth Century.* London: Routledge and Kegan Paul, 1970.

Pande, D. C. *India's Foreign Policy as an Exercise in Non-Alignment.* New Delhi: Devendra Printers, 1988.

Panikkar, K. M. *In Two Chinas, Memoirs of a Diplomat.* London: Allen and Unwin, 1955.

Pauling, Linus, ed. *World Encyclopedia of Peace.* Oxford: Pergamon Press, 1986.

Petkovic, M. "Non-Alignment and Neutrality." *Review of International Affairs* 17, no. 400 (5 December 1966): 1-2.

Pilmott, John, ed. *Vietnam: The History and the Tactics.* New York: Crescent Books, 1982.

Pinkele, Carl F. *The Sino-Soviet Territorial Dispute, 1949–1964.* New York: Praeger, 1978.

Pye, Lucian W. *China: An Introduction*, 4th ed. New York: HarperCollins, 1991.

Rajan, M. S. "The Concept of Non-Alignment and the Basis of Membership in the Movement." *Non-Alignment in Contemporary International Relations.* New Delhi, India: Vikas Publishing, 1981.

Ramazani, R. K., ed. *Iran's Revolution: The Search for Consensus.* Bloomington: Indiana University Press, 1990.

———. *Revolutionary Iran: Challenge and Response in the Middle East.* rev. ed. Baltimore, Md.: Johns Hopkins University Press, 1988.

———. *The United States and Iran: The Patterns of Influence.* New York: Praeger, 1982.

Randolph, Sean. *The United States and Thailand: Alliance Dynamics, 1950–1985.* Berkeley: University of California Press, Institute of East Asian Studies, 1986.

Rodinson, Maxime. *Europe and the Mystique of Islam.* Translated by Roger Veinus. Seattle: University of Washington Press, 1987.

Rourke. John T. International Politics on the World Stage,. 3rd ed. (Guilford, Conn.: Dushkin Publishing Group, 1991.

———. *Making Foreign Policy: United States, Soviet Union, and China.* Pacific Grove: Brooks/Cole Publishing Company, 1990.

Sachedina, Abdulaziz. *Islamic Messianism: The Idea of Mahdi in Twelver Shiaism.* Albany: State University of New York Press, 1981.

Sardesai, D. R. *Southeast Asia: Past and Present*, 2d ed. Boulder, Colo.: Westview Press, 1989.

Schurmann, Franz and Orville Schell. *Communist China: Revolutionary Reconstruction and International Confrontation (1949 to the Present.* New York: Vintage Books, 1966.

Shakori, Abolfazi. *Feqh-e Siyasi-e Islam* [Religious Politics of Islam] vol. 2. Tehran: Arin, 1982).

Shariati, Ali. *Islamshenasi* [Understanding Islam]. Mashhad, Iran: Chapkhaneh-i Tus, 1968.

Sichrousky, Harry. "Non-Alignment: Basis, History, and Prospects." *Afro-Asian and World Affairs* 2, no. 1 (Spring 1965): 19-27.

Sick, Gary. *All Fall Down: America's Tragic Encounter with Iran.* New York: Penguin Books, 1986.

Sills, David L., ed. *International Encyclopedia of the Social Sciences.* New York: Macmillan and The Free Press, 1968.

Singham, A. W. *The Non-Aligned Movement in World Politics.* Westport, Conn.: Lawrence Hill, 1977.

Singham, A. W. and Shirley Hune. *Non-Alignment in an Age of Alignments*. London: Zed Books, 1986.

Stockholm International Peace Research Institute (SIPRI). *Yearbook of World Armament and Disarmament*. London: Taylor and Francis, 1982.

Stroessinger, John G. *Nations in Darkness: China, Russia, and America,*. 5th ed. New York: McGraw-Hill, 1990.

Szulc, Tad. *Fidel: A Critical Portrait*. New York: Morrow, 1986.

Tadic, B. "Non-Alignment and Neutrality in the Contemporary World." *Review of International Affairs* 653 (5 June 1977): 11-12.

Taylor, Jay. *China and Southeast Asia: Peking's Relations with Revolutionary Movements*. 2d ed. New York: Praeger Publishers, 1976.

Thomas, Hugh S., Georges A. Fauriol, and Juan Carlos Weiss. *The Cuban Revolution Twenty- Five Years Later*. Boulder, Colo.: Westview Press, 1984.

Thompson, Kenneth W. *Cold War Theories*, vol. 1. Baton Rouge: Louisiana State University Press, 1981.

Tretiak, Daniel. *Perspectives on Cuba's Relations with the Communist System*. Ann Arbor, Mich.: Xerox University Microfilms, 1975.

U.S. Department of State. *Soviet and East European Aid to the Third World, 1981*. Washington D.C.: U.S. Government Printing Office, 1983.

Vanderlaan, Mary B. *Revolution and Foreign Policy in Nicaragua*. Boulder, Colo.: Westview Press, 1986.

Van Slyke, Lyman P. *Enemies and Friends: The United Front in Chinese Communist History*. Stanford, Calif.: Stanford University Press, 1967.

Von Glahn, Gerhard. *Law Among Nations*, 3d ed. New York: Macmillan, 1976.

Walsh, J. Richard. *Change, Continuity and Commitment: China's Adaptive Foreign Policy*. Lanham, Md.: University Press of America, 1988.

Walzer, Michael. *The Revolution of the Saints*. Cambridge: Harvard University Press, 1965.

Weinstein, Martin, ed. *Revolutionary Cuba in the World Arena*. Philadelphia: Institute for the Study of Human Issues, 1979.

Wested, Odd Arne. *Cold War and Revolution: Soviet-American Rivalry and the Origins of the Chinese Civil War, 1944-1946*. New York: Columbia University Press, 1993.

Whiting, Allen S. *China Crosses the Yalu*. Stanford, Calif.: Stanford University Press, 1960.

Wiarda, Howard J. and Harvey F. Kline, eds. *Latin American Politics and Development*, 3d ed. Boulder, Colo.: Westview Press, 1990.

Wilbur, C. Martin *Documents on Communism, Nationalism, and Soviet Advisers in China, 1918–1927*. New York: Columbia University Press, 1956.

Wilbur, C. Martin and Julie Lien-ying Howe. *Missionaries of Revolution: Soviet Advisers and Nationalist China 1920-27*. Cambridge: Harvard University Press, 1989.

Willets, Peter. "Neutrality and Non-Alignment." *Korea and World Affairs* 3, no. 3 (1971): 275-86.

———. *The Non-Aligned Movement: The Origins of a Third World Alliance*. Bombay, India: Popular Prakashan, 1978.

Williams, G. *Third-World Political Organizations*. Montclair, N.J.: Allanheld, Osmun, 1981.

Wills, John E, Jr. *Mountain of Fame: Portraits in Chinese History*. Princeton: Princeton University Press, 1994.

Wright, Robin. *Sacred Rage*, rev ed. New York: Simon and Schuster, Inc., 1986.

Wright, Thomas C. *Latin America in the Era of the Cuban Revolution*. New York: Praeger, 1991).

Wyden, Peter. *Bay of Pigs: The Untold Story*. New York: Simon & Schuster, 1979.

Yodfat, A. Y. *The Soviet Union and Revolutionary Iran*. New York: St. Martin's Press, 1984.

Young, K. J. *Negotiating with the Chinese Communist: the United States Experience, 1953–1967*. New York: McGraw-Hill, 1968.

Zabih, S. *The Mossadeqh Era*. Chicago: Lakeview Press, 1982.

Zasloff, Joseph J. *Apprentice Revolutionaries: The Communist Movement in Laos, 1930–1985*. Stanford, Calif.: Hoover Institute, Stanford University Press, 1986.

Zhisui, Li. *The Private Life of Chairman Mao: The Memoirs of Mao's Personal Physician Dr. Li Zhisui*. Translated by Tai Hung-chao. New York: Random House, 1989.

INDEX

About the Author

HOUMAN A. SADRI is Assistant Professor of International Relations at the University of Central Florida in Orlando. Previously, he taught at the University of Richmond in Virginia.

ISBN 0-275-95321-1